WAR
Memories

BY IAN BILLINGSLEY

This book is dedicated to the wonderful memory of my father - 'SAM'.

War Memories - 1995

© *This edition:*   AURORA PUBLISHING

ISBN: 1 85926 064 0

Distributed by: Aurora Enterprises Ltd.
                     Unit 9, Bradley Fold Trading Estate,
                     Radcliffe Moor Road,
                     Bradley Fold,
                     BOLTON BL2 6RT
                     Tel: 01204 370753/2 Fax: 01204 370751

Author: Ian Billingsley,
                     The author wishes to thank Mr. Lee Beth
                     and staff of the Access Centre, Partington,
                     for their help and encouragement.

Edited by: Dawn Robinson-Walsh

Printed
and bound by: MFP Design & Print,
                     Unit E3, Longford Trading Estate,
                     Thomas Street,
                     Stretford,
                     Manchester M32 0JT.

Front cover: Peace keeping pickets during the riots between the
                     Indian residents and the Burmese - Rangoon (1938-39)

Introduction

When I finally arrived at that magic age of 18, I was at last, officially old enough to have a drink with my father in the company of the people and at the place where he felt welcome......Urmston Royal British Legion.

In those days, it was a family club. All the old (maybe that should read ex.) forces men and women gathered here, week after week, month after month, year after year. It was their club. They had fought for it, and they made sure they enjoyed it.

It was here that he and his mates used to reminisce about their youth. A very special youth, with many strange and wonderful tales that used to keep my imagination captivated for ages. My youth in comparison to his, just seemed so incredibly dull. Here I was at 18, sat in a bar in one of the most peaceful little towns in this great country of ours and not once had I ventured any further than our own beaches. Yet he and his whole generation were fighting their way across the battlefields of the world at my age; some of them at the time even younger than I, some, not destined even to reach it.

The final decision to collect all these stories was made when I lost my father in 1993, just a couple of days before his 75th Birthday. He was my hero. Not that he'd captured the whole German army single handed or anything. It was just the fact that my Dad was a soldier, and he'd fought in a war. Now he was gone and along with him, a lifetime of memories.

I will never forget him. The times we used to travel together to Rhyl during those long summer holidays of childhood in a car that was always breaking down (but my Dad could fix it.) Like the time we ran out of petrol and he had to suck the fuel back up the petrol pipe. I remember how he cursed under his breath when he swallowed some for his troubles. And how he laughed when he saw the look of horror on my face as he lit up a cigarette afterwards. I was frightened he was going to blow up... he was in tears. I'll never forget that day in the car park of Queensferry Royal British Legion.

I can also remember the time he chased me from our house for a good two miles until he finally caught me. He wouldn't give up. I got a well deserved pasting for being cheeky to my Mum. It was because of this incident that I got to see the first of many of his running medals that he had won whilst he was in the Army. I used to think he was an old man. He was a lot younger than I am now and he must certainly have been a great deal fitter.

Back in Urmston Royal British Legion, in each and every corner, there is a different story being told. It's a little like now. I'm sitting here on my own in my little office after watching the anniversary of 'D-Day' Celebrations on the TV (yes, it is still 1994 here.) The stories that have been told over these past few days have been quite incredible. And there's so many of them. Wouldn't it be great if we could get them all together?

The response for this appeal alone has produced enough interesting material for at least four books of this size. And believe me, trying to select a specified

Introduction

number to start the series, was almost made with a pin. If yours isn't in this one "don't miss next week's exciting episode," as they say. There are many more to come. Still so many more to be heard and now at long last, to be remembered forever in print. This book is a tribute to its authors and I'm sure, a treasured possession for each of their families. It is just an insight into some of the incredible acts of bravery, that had become just another way of life for them.

Because of stories like these, I learned about my father 'the man.' The terrible things he'd endured, the frightening things he'd seen, and the way that he'd learned to live with the horrors that he must have witnessed during his first impressionable years of adulthood. He wasn't bitter, he didn't hate anyone, and most of all, as far as he was concerned, the world didn't owe him anything. He did what was asked of him. He wasn't alone.

Here is a generation who had lost the freedom of their youth, so that mine, and my children's generation, and hopefully many more, could enjoy theirs. They gave it up for us, and what's more, they were proud to.

This book is written by people like my father. It is a book just about people like my father. Just simple, ordinary everyday people, with just a little tale to tell. Some very well written. Some not so well written. Who cares? Some are factual accounts of battles and incidents. Others are just very personal memories of a time in a life so long ago.

I can assure you, these times really happened. Some I'm sure, slightly dusty with the passing of age and some, I'm even more certain, are very understated. Yet each and every one of them touching and most definitely lived through. And more importantly, each one, is written by a hero in his or her own right.

Please enjoy them and spare a thought for what these people went through. A word of thanks and a sincere show of gratitude for what they gave up for us, would I'm sure, be appreciated. A cheery word and a friendly smile, five minutes of your time. It's nothing to ask is it? After all, you might just learn something.

I must also add my sincere condolences to the families of....

MR J.R. LANCASTER
STAXTON, NORTH YORKSHIRE.

MR W. (BILL) SCULLY
BRADFORD, WEST YORKSHIRE.
(8TH ARMY)

two of our contributors, who sadly died before actually seeing their respective stories finally get into print.

Ian Billingsley.

Contents

Letter from
Mr. Norman Wisdom

Dear Ian,

I wish you luck with your book.

I was happy to serve in HM Forces and I had the good fortune to be in The Band of The 10th Royal Hussars in India when I was only a teenager. Fate was kind and made me lucky.

I could enjoy football, cricket, swimming, athletics and gymnastics. In fact, any sport you could think of. Smashing food, my own bed, and most important of all, wonderful mates.

I then got into the Concert Party and you probably know the rest. I can assure you, that I owe every step of my happy career to the army.

With kindest regards and best wishes.
Yours, most sincerely

NORMAN WISDOM

From World War I - World War II

CHAPTER 1

Clement James Drummond Smith was nineteen years old when he enlisted in South Australia as a signaller in the tenth Infantry Brigade. A.I.F. in 1914.

He sailed in convoy with three other troopships to Alexandria. From there, he was sent to Gallipoli but because he was ordered to remain on ship to keep contact with those men who went ashore, he was still on board next day when the ship was turned into a hospital ship to take 695 wounded and dying men back to Egypt.

From there, he was sent to France where he endured the hell of the trenches; mud, rats, lice and the shelling and deprivation of all comforts until the end of the War.

Here is a story taken from his memoirs on his twenty third birthday:

"During the night, we were to take our cable wagon to Zillebede bund or lake, with necessary requisites. A company of Engineers was to launch a pontoon for us. We were to row and lay a cable to Hillebast Corner thence by short land line to Artillery positions. This method of laying through the lake, minimised breakage by shellfire, but if broken by heavies, we would have a bigger problem for repair work.

So much for plans. By about 2300hrs on the Ypres-Lille road, Jerry had concentrated his artillery upon the intersection to intercept our artillery column on their inevitable route. The shelling

The Horse

mounted to a barrage with heavy artillery and gas shells. Soon the roadway became a stream of wagons, mules, ambulances with blockages caused by dead horses and men on the road and bridge over the canal. Other panic stricken horses refused to pass the corpses of their own species.

We donned our helmets and pressed on until the gas assumed proportions resembling heavy fog. My mount began to cough and sneeze. Every means was used by our horses to show their resentment and fear of going forward. These noble creatures knew the dread and terror of war as well as any human.

I walked out to make enquiries of the men who had negotiated that dreadful stretch. Grim stories were related by unnerved men.

Frenzied riderless horses galloped past, back to their own lines, the only home these poor creatures from many lands knew. Some appeared to be striped with black and white as the blood ran in small streams through the foam on their bodies.

There was a small break in the traffic, when we heard the sound of galloping hooves, coming towards us from the bridge. It was a riderless charger. I ran and shouted to stay his panic and he came to an abrupt halt facing me at the ditch and hedge at the side of the road.

I'll never forget him, though it was too dark to say if his colour was bay or chestnut. He had four white legs and a blaze from eyes to nostrils. A splendid English thoroughbred. Did he realise a sympathetic hand patting his neck and down his heaving flanks? He quietened down a lot and seemed loathe to leave me. I was tempted to lose my own horse and claim him for my own, but I knew I could not do it. He had rested and become calm when I bade him go adrift upon his own initiative.... from whence he'd come."

From 1914 to late 1917, he was never allowed leave for more than a couple of days away from his regiment. Then he went to London and Scotland to visit the land of his forefathers.

Clement James Drummond Smith was twice commissioned in the field when other Officers were killed. He went back to Australia with a great love of life. He trained many young volunteers in the 9th Light Horse between the two Wars and went back with many of these boys when they were sent to the Middle East. Because of his age, he was an escort for reinforcements only, much to his chagrin, as he felt he would have been valuable because of his previous experience. He spent his life helping others, particularly War Widows and Legacy Children..... he eventually died from cancer.

Mrs C.F. Padman
(niece)

"There are many reasons why a man, or these days a woman, joins the Army. Mine was a simple case of a stolen bike.

It was late 1931, and the country was in a deep recession. We were living in Yiewsley, near Uxbridge, Middlesex. My mother had recently died. There being six of us children, my father, who ran a little plumbing and decorating business with another chap, was obliged to put the four youngest into homes.

My eldest sister who was eighteen and myself aged seventeen managed to obtain some lodgings in the area. I was on piecework at a factory in Hayes called X Chair which made garden furniture, and my job was tacking the canvas on deck chair rowels, for which I earned the princely sum of a penny a dozen. I paid my landlady 12/6 a week and when she suggested that if I could find another to share my room, I need only pay 10/-, I found a lad a bit older than myself, who had come up from Wales and had a job but nowhere to live. All went well until after Christmas, when he upped and left taking my most valued possession, my bike.

Naturally, I was extremely depressed over this as it meant having to walk about four miles to and from work. My factory job was hard enough and having to walk eight miles each day made it harder so I decided to join the Army although still only seventeen.

The nearest barracks to Yiewsley was Hounslow Cavalry Barracks, so having made my decision, I walked the five or so miles to Hounslow. Arriving at the barracks I was directed to the recruiting office where I found two fellows already waiting, both Irish.

One spoke: "What are you joining?" "The army, of course," I replied. "Yes, but what regiment?", he said. "I have no idea. Why, what are you joining?" "We are joining the 8th Hussars, a good regiment. Why not come with us?" So I agreed that I would.

The recruiting Sergeant arrived complete with red, white and blue rosette in his cap, and after a few questions and a brief medical by the M.O. he said "Now then, let's see. Where can I put you?" At this point one of the Irishmen replied: "We are going into the 8th Hussars or we are walking out." "What, all of you?" he asked." "Yes, all three of us", we replied. After reflection, the Sergeant said, "Then you give me no alternative." So we received documents and travel warrants for Aldershot and the 8th King's Royal Irish Hussars.

On arrival, we were shown into a room situated above the stables where there were about thirty or so fold-up iron beds with blankets and sheets folded on top of each other. We were allocated ours. That evening I had a good talk with the fellow in the next bed who seemed to be a bit older than the rest of us. He said that he only 'wintered' in the army and would be off as soon as the weather got warmer,

The Cavalry

which true enough, he was.

The next morning we were given gym kit, boots, socks, pullover, shirts, vests and the forage hat, also two brown canvas suits; the jacket came down to my knees and the trousers had to be folded up at the bottoms to fit. Having donned these, we were introduced to the stables where several lads were busy taking the wet straw outside to dry, and shovelling and wheeling the manure to the manure heaps. " What are you standing there for?" bawled the troop Sergeant. His name was 'Jigger' Lee. "I haven't a tool, Sergeant," I replied. "So what's wrong with your hands?", he replied. At which point I had to embrace the wet straw and take it outside, which didn't do much for my canvas suit I can tell you.

I also helped water and feed the horses. In the afternoon we had to go to school for an hour, and for the rest of the day we again helped water and feed the horses, then cleaned our boots. They had to be boned using a bone-handled toothbrush, till they shone brilliantly.

On the third morning we were awakened before six and on parade in our gym kit, shivering and awaiting roll call, wanting to be on the move. P.T was followed by 'stables', sounded by the orderly trumpeter, and reputed to be one of the longest and most tuneful calls in the cavalry.

A break was called at about 10.30hrs and I thought I would try the NAAFI, situated at the far end of the drill square. Unfortunately, at the time, there were some squads being drilled. Having reached about halfway, I heard a shout: "Hey you". Not thinking that anyone would want me, (not even my mother, God bless her), and still dressed in my, by now, dirty canvas suit, I walked on. Again came the shout: "Hey you", but this time it was much louder, at which point I looked round and saw a smartly uniformed Sergeant-Major pointing his stick at me. "Yes you, at the double, and where do you think you are going?" he enquired. "To the NAAFI, Sir." I replied. "What! In that state, and when did you last clean your boots?" "This morning Sir." By the time he had finished 'dressing me down' I felt as if I had just crawled out from the manure heap. Then he asked: "How long have you been in the army?" To which I replied: "Three days, Sir."

He gave me that knowing look that we all learn to recognise after a while, and then said: "Well, what's the name of the Officer over there?" "Don't know, Sir." "What! three days and you don't know the names of the Officers of the regiment that you are in?" I thought to myself, that if I didn't even know the name of the fellow in the next bed to me, what chance had I got of knowing the names of the Officers? "Ask him then, and don't forget to salute," said the Sergeant-Major.

I marched over to where the immaculately dressed Officer was standing, his riding boots

The Cavalry

gleaming in the sunshine. Having never saluted before, I gave it my best effort. "Good Heavens! What are you doing on the square?" said this gloriously attired God. "The Sergeant-Major over there said I was to get your name, Sir." I replied. "Which Sergeant-Major?" he enquired. "That one over there, Sir." I said pointing. "What's his name?" he asked. By now I was quite unhappy. "Don't know, Sir." "Well, you had better get his name first. Go back and ask him." I returned to the Sergeant-Major who, for a while, ignored me. Then he turned. "You still here?" he asked. "Didn't you get the Officer's name?" "No, Sir." I answered sheepishly. "Why not?" he demanded. "Because he said that I have to have yours first, Sir." "My name is (and here he visibly swelled) Regimental Sergeant-Major O'Shaughnessy, and don't bloody well forget it! Now go back and ask him."

Once more I presented myself in front of the Officer and gave him my imperfect salute. "Regimental Sergeant-Major O'Shaughnessy, has asked me to get your name, Sir," I said. "Very well, soldier. My name is Captain Harbord. Now get the hell off this square as quick as you can," he ordered. I most gladly did.

It was not long before we were issued with our uniforms. SD cap and tunic, complete with riding breeches and puttees. Of course we were also given a rifle and a sword. It was now our turn to start square-bashing, sword drill and musketry. A 'dummy horse' was brought out saddled to show us the items of saddlery and their uses. We also had to learn the correct method of mounting.

This we did by taking turns. When my turn came. There was a noise like an explosion, possibly a car backfiring, and the horse bolted with me hanging on like grim death. Not knowing how to stop it, the horse careered at full gallop round the barracks and in taking a short cut round the stables it suddenly slid, the horse going one way and me another. I landed against the stable wall. Battered and bruised, I recovered, collected the horse and led him back to the party. "Who told you to dismount?" came the time-honoured question from the Sergeant. "No-one Sergeant." "Never mind," he said, looking the horse over for any injuries, "At least it shows you have guts. Take the horse back to the stables and unsaddle him."

Soon after this incident, a party of about fifteen of us started riding school in a large indoor meage complete with a rough-riding Sergeant. Surveying us, he said: "Before I start, does anyone know anything about horse-riding?" Three put up their hands. One had been a groom, one an apprentice jockey, and the third a farm-hand. "Right, stand fast you three and fall out the rest. Go and stand in a corner. I would like to see what these three can do. Three unsaddled horses were led in. They just had reins over their necks. The three lads were then ordered to mount. Not having realised that they

The Cavalry

were expected to jump up on their horses, they made several vain attempts and failed. They were used to saddles and stirrups.

"What's the matter?" asked the rough-riding Sergeant. "Don't you know how to mount? Never mind, I'll give you a lift up."

Once mounted, they were ordered to fold their arms and with a slap on the horses' rumps, it was not long before they all 'bit the dirt'. "Right, fall in everybody. Now, it is fully understood that nobody here knows sweet bugger all about horse riding. Now I can get started," he said.

It was many lessons later before we could master the art of riding bareback by gripping with our knees, having fallen off many times in the process. However, eventually we were each given our own horse and saddle to look after. Having reached the required standard of education, combined with a good score on the rifle range, our pay of two shillings (10p) a day (ten shillings per week after stoppages) was enhanced by three pence a day. By now we had also been taught to use the sword. Off we rode to Hounslow Heath to complete our training.

The regiment passing over Chertsey Bridge on the march to Hounslow, October 4th, 1932

Over a period, we were taught how to jump out of the saddle and back in again at a gallop; how to remove the saddle while at the canter and hold it above our heads; how to use the straight-bladed sword against cavalry and infantry, (the latter represented by dummies) whilst jumping hedges and other natural obstacles, and finally, how to charge! This was an exhilarating, exciting, and never-to-be-forgotten experience, and thankfully, one we never had to undertake in anger.

The course had to be completed before we became trained Cavalrymen and before we were awarded our spurs. Soon after, the regiment embarked for Egypt. I was stationed here for the next five years."

MR. T. LOUCH. UXBRIDGE.

The 4/7th Dragoons

"I am an ex - cavalryman. I joined the 4/7th Dragoons in 1930, at Shorecliffe in Kent. I was paid the princely sum of two shillings a day, out of which I had to buy my cleaning kit, metal polish, boot polish, white and khaki blanco, saddle soap, brown polish and a burnisher. The food at that time was very bad. Some of the lads were so disgusted with it that they brought it to the attention of the higher-ups.

After 12 months of training, I volunteered for service abroad with the 1st Royal Dragoon Guards in India (Meerut). I began to enjoy the life, my main hobbies being football, cricket, hockey and bicycle polo, at which I was very good. The civil population weren't very welcoming towards the British soldiers and we had to be very careful when we went out in the evening.

October 1935 came, and we were ordered to pack our kit and be ready to go home. The day came and we set sail from Bombay. After a week or so we arrived at Aden, the entrance to the Red Sea where, after a couple of days, we were ordered to disembark at Port Tewfick. A train was in the station and off we went to Abersia, 2 km. out of Cairo. This was the time when Mussolini was at war with Ethiopia, and we thought that we would be involved.

The 7th Hussars were in the process of being mechanised and one of the jobs we had was to look after 500 horses until we managed to rid ourselves of them. It didn't take long and off we went via Port Said to home.

At the end of 1936 I said goodbye to the army and got a job at the colliery as an improver bricklayer. I was doing very well until War was declared with Germany and I was called to the colours.

We had horses for about twelve months in Palestine before becoming the Coastal Defence with 4/7 guns, where we transferred to Benghazi. We weren't there long before the Germans drove us back and we had to destroy our guns and make for Tobruk. We were surrounded on three sides, with the sea on the other side. The Jerries dive bombed us every hour, but we managed to hold. Eventually we got out leaving the South Africa Corps to fight on alone, but they soon surrendered.

We went to Palestine, where we trained to become Tankies. Our first battle was at Alm Alfa, where we lost a few tanks and returned to Palestine for further training. Then came the big one... ALAMEIN. The O.C. seated us all on the sand and he started to speak: "Tomorrow, we go to Tripoli".

The bombardment started at midnight, about the 23rd of October. One thousand twenty-five pounder guns were blazing away when we got the order to advance. I was driving the lead tank. We got through a mine field and all hell let loose. We could see the bullets and shells going across our front; it was dark and the missiles were white hot.

I felt a thump on the off-side of my tank and I knew that I had lost a track. We started going round and round in circles. The wireless operator came over the intercom: "Jas. Can you get us out of here?. The troop leader has been badly hit." "Sorry Leslie," I replied, "I've only one track."

Then there was silence until Jimmy Lewis's voice came over intercom. "Leslie and the troop leader are dead," he said. "There's blood all over the place," I shouted, "get out of the tank as quickly as possible, it's a death trap." I threw open my cover and got out. I lay flat on the sand. Jimmy had just cleared the turret. I shouted for him to jump, but was too late. The blast flung him off and he landed about six yards away. I thought that maybe I could help him, but he'd been killed outright.

By now it was getting lighter. Three Germans came towards me, one shouted something that I didn't understand followed by Kamerad. I knew what that meant. They searched me for weapons and then put me in a trench with one guard who could speak perfect English. We had a good conversation, all Germans weren't bad. During the day, the sun became hotter and the guard and I had no water. He was only about eighteen or nineteen years of age. As the night approached again I was moved three hundred yards further back.

The British shells were landing every second. There were five prisoners. I was going to escape. I'd noticed the guard had disappeared. I turned to a mate, Ron and said: "I'm going." He looked at me and replied: "Hold on. I'm coming with you," We left, keeping as low as possible as we ran for about three hundred yards towards a large trench. Feeling safe, I said to Ron "Try to get some sleep now." I nodded off, but Ron was concerned about the shelling. I told him not to worry as the Germans wouldn't waste shells on two men.

Later, an Officer of the Royal Horse Artillery was salvaging what he could, when he spotted us. He told us to follow him. We jumped into his five hundred weight vehicle and were taken back to his lines where he left us with a gun crew. "Get these two men a meal, a mug of tea and a packet of cigs," he ordered.

We stayed a few hours, and then I said to the Gunnery Sergeant: "I think we'll try to reach our own lines now Searg." But he told us to stay where we were. I thought different. It was my duty to get back to my own regiment, so we left.

My C.O. sent for me to ask what had happened. I told him everything; I didn't even get a pat on the back or a well done. I was back in another tank the following day. I was a reservist. We kept going to Tunisia; the Germans had finally given up.

The worst was still to come, the Invasion of France. A lot of good lads were killed during the campaign."

**JAMES (JAS) GERRARD.
TYLDESLEY. MANCHESTER.**

- 1939

"On the 10th September, 1939 I was approaching 30 years of age and was working for the Corporation Electricity Department, as a shift driver on a wage of approx £2.18 per week. Out of this I had to pay superannuation and union dues. I had been married for two years and I was buying a new house for £345.

My wife also worked as a supervisory machinist, but even so, we could never have afforded to manage on our combined wages and live decently. I played the piano three nights a week at a local pub and also attended auction salerooms in between shifts and bought vacuum cleaners, sewing machines and bric-a-brac, renovating them and selling the same for a reasonable profit. I also had a clientele of about thirty five ladies for whom I serviced vacuums and sewing machines when required.

As a corporation employee, I was informed by my manager that I would be exempt from War service. However, on the Sunday prior to the 11th September, 1939, I read in the newspapers an account of the sinking of the S.S. Athenia and of a passenger who ran around the ship to rescue his daughter then realised it was too late. She was dead.

This, plus other accounts from the survivors gave me a feeling of utter anger. So much so, that on the Monday after the 11th September, I went to the nearest recruiting centre and volunteered for

CHAPTER 2

One Man's War

War service. I was medically examined and passed fit by the doctor and told to report back the next morning at 0900 hrs and to bring some sandwiches with me.

My wife was understandably upset, and my manager called me a bloody fool; but he was proud of me. He was an ex. Captain. I reported as requested and I was made acting Warrant Officer and given custody of six other young men to take to Aldershot, where we were kitted out.

We were allowed into Aldershot at night but as we did not receive any army pay for a couple of weeks, I made a few bob playing the piano in a pub at night that was packed out with troops.

Whilst serving here, I underwent a P.T. And unarmed combat course for instructors, which I passed. Then finally we were marched to Rushmoor Arena, where we slept in the stands. We were issued with a couple of blankets each, weapons and instructions.

After meals we would wander around the company office which was surrounded by trees. It was like a little forest. Attached to these trees were speakers from which the daily orders would be issued from the Sgt. Major's office. It was quite funny to hear him bellow: "Stand still that man!" when it was quite obvious that he couldn't possibly have seen anyone, but it worked. Everyone stood still.

Finally, I was posted to the R.A.S.C. 4th Division Ammunition Company at Andover where we were billeted in tents which were erected over deep holes in the chalk. It was not long before the whole unit was infested with lice and we all had to be decontaminated, our clothes as well. We went on regular manoeuvres on Salisbury Plain where we learned to use Bren guns and small arms. Those non-drivers amongst us were given a ten day driving course.

At the end of November, we were moved to a southern port where we embarked for France. The voyage was uneventful and we did what exercise we could around the crowded decks. We landed at St. Nazaire with the British Expeditionary Force where we were billeted in a disused glass factory near the docks. We were then issued with a mug of tea and the biggest cheese sandwich you ever saw. A couple of lads lost theirs to the rats that were scuttling around all night.

The next morning we started to unload the vehicles and equipment and we started off through Nantes and Le Mans to the accompaniment of cheers and applause from the French en-route. We finally reached Arras (Pas de Calais) the scene of a big battle in World War One. It is about forty miles from the Belgian border.

On the way there, we passed many cemeteries full of the allied troops from the First World War, all uniformly laid out with white crosses. As we passed, the lads stopped their singing and were strangely quiet.

We spent the first night in a hall called the 'Salle de Fête' and next morning, came my second volunteering mistake. Our Captain asked if anyone could speak French and I was about the only one who could make myself understood. The French of my school days turned out to be nothing like the French of the 'Pas de Calais'.

I accompanied the Captain around the district where at each house I asked the occupants if they could house any soldiers for which they would be paid 'X' francs per day. At the end of four hours we managed to house about seventy troops and Officers and the rest of the company set to, packing palliasses with straw.

Our next step was to position the lorries at strategic points close to the billets and load off the ammunition onto the pavements and organise a twenty four hour guard. Beside doing the vehicle maintenance, we also had to dig slit trenches all around. We dug up quite a few relics of the first war: helmets, swords and the bones of a donkey.

I was up on orders to receive a Lance Corporal's stripe and a week later given a further stripe to be made a fully paid up corporal. It was on being promoted that I realised that the welfare of the lads was all important and I vowed to give it my all. After all, I was thirty years old and the others were all teenagers.

I was issued with a motorcycle and given charge of a section of seven lorries, carrying gun cotton, molotov cocktails and a Bren gun, rifle and revolver ammunition. I had sixteen drivers and four loaders in my section. Apart from the four loaders and myself, being so young, they all took it as some sort of picnic.

We were allowed into Lille on pass and I recall an amusing incident. Outside one of the brothels there was a whitewashed sign which read: 'Anglais Soldats visit here. It is the place your fathers visited in 1914/18'. Some wag had added 'same staff'.

I also visited Ypres, the scene of two big battles in World War I, where the trenches and dugouts had been preserved; guarded by the ghosts of thousands of allied troops, lying in neat rows of well looked after graves with regulation white crosses near by. This is the place, I was told, that one Christmas hostilities ceased for a few hours and the two sides made contact and shook hands until resuming the fight the next day. Here I must pay tribute to the French for the regular maintenance of these cemeteries.

I managed to get up a fairly creditable concert party here and we gave several shows to units round about until one day it was announced that Gracie Fields was coming to give a show at the Round Theatre (Roubaix) which was in Lille, only one mile from the Belgian border.

The show was only for selected troops from the surrounding units and I was selected to go. The concert party had already given one show here and due to the late arrival of Gracie's party, the Captain and I managed to round them up to stand in for her until she arrived.

We were welcomed onto the stage to the accompaniment of loud cheers. Keeping going until she finally arrived at 2245 hrs. Gracie kept everybody happy by singing her little heart out until gone midnight. I was introduced to her whilst I was backstage, thanked for my help and invited for drinks with her party and the Officers. I finally left at 0200 hrs in the O/C's jeep.

One day we received a signal from G.H.Q. to the effect that all Officers were to be able to ride a motorcycle. I was given the unenviable task of teaching one junior Officer. I picked a 500cc Triumph as being the most suitable and as he had ridden a pushbike previously, that made things a little easier. I started off by putting the bike up on its stand and getting him acquainted with the gears, etc.

The lesson was taken in a quadrangle behind the company office and he had his first attempt at riding around the yard. In the centre of the yard there was a pile of empty petrol cans. Yes, you've guessed it! Half way around he lost his balance and landed in the middle of them; much to the amusement of the Company Officer who was watching from his window.

We had two dispatch riders who were inseparable pals.

Night driving was always hazardous due to the poor lighting because of the blackout. The lorries only had a small light underneath the back which used to shine onto a white spot on the axle. It was always difficult to ascertain just how far away you were from these vehicles. One of these poor lads must have judged the light wrong one night and he hit the back of the lorry. He was killed outright.

When the Germans commenced hostilities, they bombed the cinema in Arras. We rounded up all the company and in the space of two hours, we were loaded up and on our way into Belgium.

The 2nd May, we were greeted with cascades of flowers and cheers from the Belgian people as we entered Brussels. We were deployed around the town square and I couldn't help noticing just what a lovely, clean place it was, all snow white buildings.

The lads kipped down in the lorries and I mounted a guard on the same. I was approached by a lady who spoke perfect English. I found out that she hailed from the same district as I did. She had married a French Officer just after the First World War. She then invited me into her home for coffee and biscuits and we had a good chat about our home town. She also made a large jug of coffee for the lads on guard.

We only stayed there one night. The following morning saw us on our way to Leuven and then towards Genk near the German frontier. Before we reached the town, a dispatch rider arrived with a message. I wasn't to carry on any further. Instead, I was to proceed immediately to Mechalin (Malines) heading away from the frontier.

During this time, we were subjected to spasmodic hedgehopping raids which made moving during the day very difficult. We travelled by night. From this point on, I never saw an Officer but received all my instructions from dispatch riders as to which map reference I should move to. My last instruction was to load off all my ammunition in a field for the Royal Engineers to blow up and to destroy my vehicles. This I did, keeping only one lorry and a Bren gun. We all travelled in this, living off the land as we went. My orders stated that it was now a case of 'every man for himself.'

We were on the outskirts of Kortrick near Menen, West Flanders and from here I took a route towards Poperinge and at one halt I went foraging for food in a deserted farm. There were a few cows that had not been milked for days so I brought the lads to the farm and we helped ourselves to a gallon or two. We also caught a couple of hens and in the cellar we found a stack of potatoes. We boiled it all up in a tin bath and had ourselves a feast.

One night, we were hiding under some trees only to be awoken by a loud croaking noise. The noise was coming from dozens of frogs (or toads) we didn't get any more sleep that night. The following morning we dammed the brook until we had about four feet of water and all had a damned good soak.

As we neared Poperinge we could see a huge pall of smoke and flames, so I left the lorry and the lads and went to see if we could get through. Things seemed to be O.K. As we approached the main square, standing in amongst the rubble was a Military Policeman. He gave us instructions to follow a route which he had marked out with blitzed timber, etc. We followed it around the town towards Dunkirk which was taking a terrible hammering from the Germans. It was at this point that a dispatch rider approached us and he advised us to skip Dunkirk and head for La Panne a few miles further up the coast. I took his advice.

We came to a bridge where the R.E.s had mined ready to blow up. There was a rifle brigade deployed on the opposite bank. It was deemed most urgent that we should get across as soon as possible because the Germans were only a few miles away and their shells were getting awfully close. We moved damned quick.

We arrived on the beach at 1500 hrs to be greeted by an Officer who ordered us to fall in behind a column of boys waiting for boats to come in. I was then told to follow him to help keep order amongst all the men (French and Belgians) who were also hoping to get off the beach. We had a little trouble from them because they were not allowed to embark whilst our lads were still there.

One Man's War

One or two tried to board boats by wearing allied battle dress. One can only guess where they obtained them.

There were only two small ships close to the water's edge when we arrived, and some of the lads were on the verge of hysteria as the German planes strafed the beach quite often. I saw but one British plane during the five days I spent there and he was shot down into the sea by German fighters.

As the planes attacked, a Staff Officer lying on his belly on the sand, was hit by a bullet. It went through the back of his thigh leaving a nasty hole in the front. A Sergeant and myself carried him to the makeshift medical unit set up in a bombed out outhouse. He ordered us to get him aboard the next possible boat as he had some vital information to give. We found a small rowing boat in the shed, so off we rowed, out towards the waiting ships. We put him aboard and went back to the beach.

That same afternoon during another attack, I was blown several yards up the beach as the planes dropped anti-personnel bombs on us. I remember being carried up to the medical unit and also getting a jab. I next remember coming to on a small boat out at sea. It all seemed so unreal to me that voyage. I just had this strange feeling of peace. We were diverted to Ramsgate by a patrol boat as we neared the English coastline and we were then carried ashore to the waiting ambulances. I have never seen so much chocolate or cigarettes as I saw that day on the quayside."

An extract from the war memoirs of Mr. Jack Gardner entitled:

'ONE MAN'S WAR'

- 1940

CHAPTER 3

"As I left home on the morning of 5th Feb. 1940, I said cheerio to my mum. There were tears in her eyes as I said: "See you soon. It will all be over in six months." Little did I know, that as I reached the top of the road to turn and wave, that the next time I would see her would be a long four years away. I had already said goodbye to my girlfriend Peggy. She was to wait all those years for me to come home.

I caught a train at Watford Junction for Farnborough to join the Royal Tank Corps. I arrived sometime in the afternoon and immediately started my six months training. It was quite an experience for me as I met people from all walks of life and needless to say, I made some great friends. As far as the training went, it made a great change from printing. I had only just finished my apprenticeship at the Sun Engraving Company. I passed out after six months as a tank driver and wireless operator.

November 1940 saw me billeted at East Grinstead. Whilst there, Peggy came to see me (was I happy). They were two great days. I travelled from there to Liverpool en-route to North Africa. We boarded the 'Reino del Pacifico,' having one torpedo scare before docking at Port Tufik seven weeks later.

We were then put on a train bound for the Sudan being bombed by a lone Italian plane as we travelled. It scored two direct hits killing several Indians that were travelling with us. Arriving at

Tanks

Agordat, we unloaded the tanks without any aggro. We were then to make our way to Keren, a town held by the Italians. Our infantry were having trouble shifting them and had asked for tank support. It took us just two to three days to get them moving. To be quite honest, the baboons that inhabited the rocky hills gave us more trouble. They would get in our way and we didn't have the heart to hurt them.

Leaving Keren on our way to Asmara, I've never seen as many condoms as left by the retreating Italians. I never did find out why they needed them, as women were very scarce around here.

After two or three weeks I landed in Alexandria, Egypt. After my first taste of war, I was given a few days leave to go into Cairo. That was an experience. Especially round the back alleys and side streets. Mind you I was never alone. I always had my mates with me and we were armed. After this short spell, which included a short refit for the tanks, we were ready for the Libyan Desert.

We arrived at Mersa Matru, our camp, in early June 1941. It wasn't long before we had orders to move up to the front line.

It's funny, but none of us seemed scared. Each tank crew was given a packet of cigs and a bottle of beer as we moved off. It was slow progress as the tanks would only travel at 10mph. We arrived at what they called the 'wire' that divided Egypt and Libya. There were gaps every quarter of a mile.

It was now 05.00 hrs, on the 7th July, 1941. We had waited through the previous night watching the German flares. It was like a firework display. By the time morning came they knew exactly where we were. At 05.30 hrs., we received the order to attack; what a fiasco. We never stood a chance. We had 25 ton Matilda tanks (the biggest in the army) 2 pounder guns and a Bren machine gun. Twelve tanks against the Jerry Tiger tanks with 88mm guns. Each tank carried a 4 man crew.

We had only moved forward 200 yards when we were hit by an 88mm shell. Fortunately it was only a glancing blow but enough to break a track and immobilise us. We stopped and smoke was coming up through the turret. The gunner (Cyril Hook) started to climb out. I tried to stop him, but he climbed to his death. The Tank Commander told me to see if I could get anything on the radio. They were the last words he ever spoke. As he was talking he opened the turret and was killed by a piece of shrapnel. The driver and myself managed to get out unharmed by climbing out of the driving hatch instead of the turret.

Looking around it was chaos with tanks burning and bodies everywhere. An armoured car was coming towards us. I looked at my driver and said: "This is it." It stopped by us and as we surrendered, the German Officer said: "For you the War is over." I remember asking him if I could get my cigarettes from the tank. In perfect English he called over one of his men and off we went, we climbed back into the tank. I opened my locker as the German stuck a gun in my back. I retrieved my 50 Players Navy Cut and 50 Indian cigarettes (army issue); they were terrible. I expected him to take the Players but to my joy he opted for the Indian cigs. I also took a tin of Walls sausages which he let me keep (not a bad bloke really.)

We were taken to Bardia for interrogation; there were 22 of us from various tanks. They wanted to know of our strengths and the capability of the tanks. I don't know why because when I went before the German Officer he knew more than I did. He had more Leyland handbooks than I had ever seen.

FROM BARDIA TO BENGHAZI.

I wasn't sorry to leave Bardia as the Royal Navy started shelling it just before we left. It sounded like double decker buses going over. The Germans handed us over to the Italians whose job it was to take us to Benghazi. What a trek. We were put into open lorries with planks of wood for seats. We had water but no food and the Italians took great delight in putting bayonets to our throats and calling us English bastards.

On our arrival at Benghazi, we were taken to a German working camp. There were already 300 prisoners there. We were given a meal of Erzatz bread, sauerkraut and coffee. Three of my mates and I often talked of escaping but always came to the conclusion that it would be impossible here in the desert. We would just have to bide our time.

After a night's rest we were all given our various duties which involved cleaning the German barracks, the food stores and loading trucks for the front line (which was strictly against the Geneva Convention) with oil and petrol at a station just outside Benghazi.

Those that looked the fittest were picked for the oil dump. I was one of this team totalling roughly thirty. We were taken to the dump by lorries. Our task was to load 50 gallon oil drums and large cans of petrol on to the lorries. The oil drums were spaced 50 yards apart because of the bombing. It was hard work pushing them through the sand to the ramps.

We still did our bit. The guards were quite a distance away and couldn't see us. We unscrewed the stoppers on the barrels with a wrench that we had pinched from a lorry, all the oil drained out into the sand and we put the empty barrels onto the lorries. We made out they were heavy as we lifted them on. This must have had some effect at the front line as the German supplies were very limited. After a few weeks I was transferred to the food stores.

This was a better job. We were loading food for

25

Tanks

the front line at Tobruk. As the guards were few, we would go round the back of the stacks, slide the top off the boxes and puncture as many tins as possible and replace the top ready for loading. You can imagine the result. We of course ate well.

We were always searched before we went back to camp, so we had the idea of tying a sock between our legs with a piece of string around our waist, which was used to carry a tin out. Sometimes even chocolate. Because it dangled between our legs we got away with it, as the guards never touched there.

This went on for some time until one of the gang got greedy and put two tins in. After being searched we were walking away and he started clanging. We were called back and searched again. The secret was out. The German Officer must have had a sense of humour; he just laughed, took our tins and let us go.

I had now been in Benghazi for five and half months and was now assigned to barrack cleaning. I became friendly with a German whilst doing this work and he took a liking to me. Every morning he would give me scraps of food, talk about his family and more importantly update me on the happenings at the Front.

The Germans were being pushed back, mainly due to lack of supplies. This, of course, was good news. It was obvious our army was getting closer as we were being bombed almost every night by our own planes. On one of these raids the German barracks was hit killing many, including my friend.

On the 24th December 1941, the Germans were becoming excited. Our boys were on the outskirts of Benghazi, and we were all looking forward to being liberated, but the Germans had other ideas. On the 26th December we embarked on an Italian cruiser and taken to Brindisi, Italy.

MY CAPTIVITY IN ITALY

On our arrival at Brindisi, we were taken to a makeshift camp of tents. It had been snowing and it was bitterly cold. All we had on was our tropical clothes. We were given a bread roll and coffee; we were starving. We stayed in this field, under canvas for four days.

We were then put on a train bound for Porto St Giogio. Our next camp had a head count of one thousand, five hundred prisoners already there. I remember walking through the streets to the camp, being jeered at, jostled and stoned by the town folk, arriving at the camp for the start of a new year 1942.

Each hut housed 200 prisoners; we slept in bunks. I slept on top, a chap named Walter Walton had the bottom bunk. We became good pals sharing what food we had. The beds were infested with woodlice.

About the middle of February I was seriously ill with pleurisy, and spent four weeks in the camp hospital (if you could call it that).

As the weather started to improve there was talk of escaping. Twenty airforce prisoners decided that our bunk was the best location to start digging the tunnel under. They dug for five weeks replacing the concrete slabs when the guards were due. It was never found until 18 airmen had escaped. I had the opportunity to go with Wally, but declined. All the airmen were recaptured.

After several months we were moved again, this time to a camp at Masserata, still on the Adriatic. I became friendly with three chaps who were very eager to escape. This was the best opportunity I'd had so far.

About the end of August 1943, there were rumours of a landing by our forces at Salerno. On September 3rd 1943, all the guards had disappeared, so I said to my three mates: "let's go." At 1100 hrs, we broke down the door and we were away. We ran expecting a bullet in the back, but nothing happened.

We came to a farm and to our surprise, we were offered food and wine. We were then told that Italy had capitulated and they were on our side (but beware of the Fascists, as I was to find out later). We were the only ones to escape, as the others in the camp were taken to Germany the very next day.

We slept under haystacks, scrounging food as we made our way south. We heard that the Fascists were looking for us; they had put posters up in the villages telling people not to help the escaped prisoners. Apparently, quite a few had escaped from up north and were making their way south also. We talked and decided that it was now too dangerous to stay together, so we went our separate ways. There, I was on my own, in a hostile country, but I coped.

I never did see any of these three again. When I became desperate, throwing caution to the wind I stopped at a farm. Luckily, they gave me food and drink, because their son had come home from the army. According to him all the Italians threw down their weapons and went home. They made me very welcome and I was to stop there on and off for 8 months.

It had become almost impossible for me to head south towards Naples because of the retreating Germans. I joined the Partisans along with the son of these people. About twelve of us would go out at night, placing barriers across the main roads to stop the Germans. The Italians looked after me well.

I was lying in bed one day when they woke me to say that the Germans were coming to the house. I dressed quickly and jumped out of the back bedroom window, and hid until I got the all clear. After a couple of months, I went down with malaria. Our troops were in the vicinity now, so the son

Tanks

Watford Parish Church - 4th December 1944. R.B.Watson and wife Margaret.

contacted them saying that a British soldier was staying with them and that he had contracted malaria. An ambulance was sent for me and I was taken to hospital in Porto St Giogio. I remember the tears that flowed as I left. I felt very sad. After all, they had in effect saved my life.

After two days in hospital I was flown to Bari for further treatment. I was treated with quinine for about three weeks and recovered. When discharged, I was given a rail pass to Naples. I sat on a seat in Garibaldi Square to read my instructions again, when two American soldiers sat beside me. We were chatting. When I told them that I had escaped from a POW camp, they were amazed. They couldn't do enough for me. I was taken back to their barracks and introduced to their Commanding Officer. I was treated like royalty. They even laid on a staff car to take me the rest of my journey to Resina. I left promising to return one day, but sadly, I never did.

When I arrived at my new camp, I was completely kitted out with a new uniform, including a greatcoat. I kicked my heels for two days only to be told that I wouldn't get a boat to England for at least one month. I decided to ask for permission to visit the family at the farm but this was refused point blank. I wasn't happy. Deciding to go anyway, I jumped out of a side window to avoid the MPs on the gate, and hitch hiked back to the farm. I stayed for two months missing my boat home.

I left early November 1944, making my way to Naples via Rome. Having hitched a lift to Rome, I stopped a car on the Rome to Naples road. It was the Military Police. I explained that I was going to Resina. Without any fuss, they made arrangements for me to stop at their camp overnight. They then took me back to Resina the next day.

I arrived in quite a state. Gone was the newly issued uniform they had supplied me with last time I was here. All I had now was a dirty old pair of trousers, worn out shoes and shirt, and an old hat. I looked like a tramp. After telling them who I was they put me straight into the cells.

Next morning after another refit, I was told that I was on a charge.... Desertion. This was obviously ridiculous. When I was marched before the CO, he asked me what I had to say. After explaining about my escapades in the desert, and how I managed to escape from the POW camp, he shook my hand and said that I deserved a holiday. He wished me luck. Nothing was ever mentioned about my clothes.

There was a ship in Naples Harbour that was to take me home. I finally arrived in Liverpool via Gibraltar. It was November 1944. I was informed that my final destination was to be Amersham, Bucks. I was elated. It was only four miles from my home. No sooner had I arrived, than I was on a bus to Watford. When I knocked on the door, after four years away from home, there wasn't any reply. Of course they weren't expecting me, they didn't even know that I was in England.

A neighbour informed me that they were all at a wedding for the day. It wasn't far away so off I went. When the family saw me, everything stopped. What a reunion. Even my girlfriend Peggy was there. We were married on the 2nd December, 1944.

I was demobbed in Northampton in March 1946, after serving my time in Germany. There are many that served their country and suffered more than I did. I was lucky. I, at least, have lived to have and enjoy my family."

**Ex Sergeant RB Watson 7906725
Royal Tank Corps.**

**This story he dedicates to his
granddaughter, Mandy Reed.**

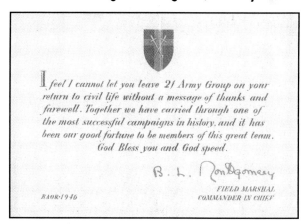

I feel I cannot let you leave 21 Army Group on your return to civil life without a message of thanks and farewell. Together we have carried through one of the most successful campaigns in history, and it has been our good fortune to be members of this great team. God Bless you and God speed.

B. L. Montgomery

FIELD MARSHAL
COMMANDER IN CHIEF

BAOR·1946

The Escape

"As a twenty-one year old soldier I was taken prisoner by the Germans in Belgium at 18:00 hours on Sunday 26 May, 1940 and taken to a camp at Dortmund from where after a few days I escaped.

After three days, I was captured and ended up with a lot of other prisoners in a cattle truck and transported by rail to Jorun in Poland.

Glasow - December 1945.

My camp was known as the 'Balloon Hangar' and we lived in tents. I escaped from this camp also but again was captured after six days. So that was an improvement on my previous escape.

I was then put into a Fort known as XX A, where I made my third and successful escape on Saturday 17 August, 1940.

I made my way towards Warsaw having many scary moments on the way. Some time in October, I arrived at a place called Laski which is five or six miles from Warsaw and I may add, that all along my route I had been helped by many brave Polish people who would have been shot had they been caught.

By the time I got to Laski, my socks had worn out and my heels were infected and my legs were very swollen and blue with red veins showing. I had a large lump in each groin. To slither along, I had to put my hands in my trouser pockets and press the lumps. I felt so tired I didn't care whether I was captured again.

I came across a mansion type house with a wall around it with a large pair of iron gates. I rang the bell and a boy of about fourteen years of age came to me and said something in Polish which I didn't understand. I used my two magic words -Angelski Soldat!- and the boy went back to the house and appeared with a dark haired lady who spoke English. I told her my circumstances and she opened the gate and took me in to the kitchen where she let me

The Escape

have a wash and made me some cheese sandwiches and a glass of milk.

The dark haired lady was obviously the mistress of the house and she brought a young lady who appeared to be a maid. She said something to her. The maid disappeared and then returned with a bowl of hot water and soap and then she took of my boots and stinking socks. She gently washed my feet till they were clean, then bathed my heels in fresh water and bandaged them.

In the meantime, the young lad had brought a two wheeled flat bottomed cart in the house and with the maid's help, I got on the cart and the lad drove me to a local doctor where the maid gave him a letter from her mistress.

I had to take my trousers off and after scanning me the doctor said in passable English that another forty-eight hours without attention and I would have had to have my legs amputated or die. The doctor gave me an injection in each buttock with a very large syringe.

I was then transported on the cart to a convent where the maid gave the Mother Superior another letter. I was then taken by two nuns who bathed me. I was too ill to be embarrassed.

After my bath I was put to bed in a small ward with four beds in it where I fell into a deep sleep. Whilst asleep, I dreamed that I came out of the ward in a white coat and looked down at myself on the bed. Then, I took a large saw and cut my legs off but there was no blood. I then threw the legs into a dustbin.

Moscow - July 1941.

When I awoke after two days, a nun was sat by my side bathing my fore head and taking my temperature. I think they were of the Franciscan Order as they wore brown habits.

I was with them for three weeks and then they put me in touch with the Polish Underground movement who got me to Russia where I was taken to Hubyanka prison.

I was released on the twenty fourth of June, two days after the German invasion of Russia. Afterwards I served at the British Embassy in Moscow until October 1941 when I was sent home for my own safety.

I am not a Roman Catholic nor am I very religious but whenever I think of those brave nuns I think of them as: 'Gods Angels on Earth.'"

**S. GREEN. D.C.M.
GORTON.
MANCHESTER.**

31

- 1941

CHAPTER 4

"The year: 1941. The place; just outside Gibraltar Harbour. I was serving on board HMS MALAYA, a veteran battleship of the Battle of Jutland and together with Ark Royal, we were part of force 'H' based on Gibraltar.

It was 1600 hrs on a sunny afternoon. We were returning to port having succeeded in getting three ships out of a total of eleven through to sorely pressed Malta and were almost back in harbour, with the Ark Royal on our starboard beam. This mighty ship (which was very instrumental in the sinking of the 'Bismarck') looked a majestic sight as her planes took off heading inland towards the shore base. Our escort destroyers were steaming line ahead to harbour and we took up position astern.

I was standing on top of 'B' turret, having just secured as a member of the gun's crew, when suddenly, a great explosion rent the air. There was Ark Royal with smoke billowing up from her flight deck, followed by long tongues of flames. She was soon listing at a crazy angle and the planes that had remained on deck, were now slipping into the sea.

The destroyers turned about and dropped depth charges in all directions. I was dumbfounded, but was even more so when to my amazement, I saw a periscope cutting through the still waters about one hundred yards off our starboard bow. After firing his torpedoes, the canny U-boat Captain had

Goodbye Ark Royal

taken his boat not away from the scene as expected, but right in amongst the other ships. Somewhere, an A.A. Gun opened up from the 'Malaya' on the still visible periscope. Then it disappeared.

A week later a small patrol vessel returned to Gibraltar harbour with survivors from the U-boat responsible for the sinking of that great ship HMS Ark Royal."

**JOHN F. CUNNINGHAM.
RUNCORN. CHESHIRE.**

The Promise

"The memory haunts me. The memory of a promise made to a pretty girl fifty four years ago. A promise never fulfilled.

It was in the town of Herakleion, on Crete. The month was May 1941. The German paratroopers had landed ten days ago and after hard and bitter fighting, had been driven from the town. My battalion of infantry were now holding the west end of the town with positions along the ancient Venetian wall, my own company the end nearest the sea. There was still German activity away to our front as the occasional sticks of parachutes denoted. Whether these were reinforcements or supplies, was too far away to ascertain. The area immediately to our front was still an unoccupied zone, except for the dead German, Greek and British we couldn't bury.

I was a company runner; my job was to take messages from the Company HQ to platoons and to the Battalion HQ a mile to the rear in some badly damaged houses in the town centre. I had made the trip a number of times with messages too important to trust to our single telephone wire.

Early one afternoon "Dusty Rhodes" came to me and said the line was out again and I had to go with him. There was still plenty of air activity with ME110's patrolling almost continually, diving and strafing anything that moved or gave them suspicions. Dusty followed the wire through the debris scattered streets and I kept a wary eye on the sky.

Almost half way to HQ stood a reasonably large building on the left side of the road, I had noticed particularly because of the large red cross painted on the roof. One gable had been damaged by a bomb and like the rest of the buildings seemed completely lifeless. Dusty and I had got about twenty yards past when I heard a girls voice calling: "Soldier, soldier." A girl stood on top of the stairs of the hospital. I told Dusty that I would see what she wanted and went back.

She was dressed in a brown skirt and white blouse. She was very pale and pretty. She spoke in broken English but was easily understood. "German soldiers inside," She told us. "And the doctor and his wife German. When planes come they go out back and signal with sheets." I said to Dusty: "Come on and we will see what's going on." He insisted that he had to go on and repair the wire.

I followed the girl into the little vestibule and then a rather stout woman dressed in a nurse's uniform arrived. She rattled off some Greek to the girl and then took her arm and tried to pull her through the facing door. The girl resisted and a little struggle took place, and then another woman appeared. She was smartly dressed and looked to be in her thirties; she joined in the argument, she then turned to me and tried to pull my rifle from my shoulder.

I was not having any of that and told her forcibly.

She gave up and flounced through the door and disappeared. The girl and I followed, but the nurse stayed where she was.

Through the inner door was a small hospital ward with six or eight beds down either side. It was immaculate. A highly polished wooden floor which made my army boots sound like the crack of doom. The beds had snowy white sheets and light blue counterpanes. In each bed was a man. Some were lying quite still, with only the movements of their eyes as they followed me down the ward. A few were asleep, or pretended to be. One or two were bandaged. One blonde haired lad was sitting up and he spoke as we drew level with his cot: "Hello Tommy, it will not be long now before we take all the island," he said. "You've no hope of that", I answered. He just gave a knowing grin.

At the end of the ward was another door which the girl opened. She beckoned me in, and we went down a short flight of steps. It was like descending into a sewer. The stench made me gag. A six feet wide corridor ran the length of the split level building, some thirty feet. Every available foot was taken up by people: men, women, children. Some were lying on blankets others were sitting against the wall. Some women were nursing children but all were deadly quiet. An old man gave me a feeble smile and a child whimpered as it's mother clutched it to her.

There were doors on either side, all open to

The Promise

show tiny rooms all crammed with figures. Some had dirty bandages on their heads and limbs. In others were bare cots with two or three people lying on top. The whole place was badly lit and it was difficult not to stumble over the bodies.

The girl went to the end of the passage where an open door led to a small enclosed courtyard. Along one wall was a mountain of filth and rubbish. Empty tins, filthy rags and blood stained bandages. Lying on the heap was a man dressed in British Battle Dress. I ran across to him and the girl called out "Italiano prisoner". I knew there were some prisoners on the island but since the early days when I saw them being brought ashore and then herded in ragged columns away from the docks, I had not seen any. The man was dead, and not too recently either.

Going back up the stairs the girl halted. "You bring British?", she asked. I was choked and could barely speak: "Have no soldiers seen this?" She looked at me and said: "Nobody come."

I stamped my feet down hard as I went back down the ward. If any of the Jerries were actually sleeping, I wanted them awake and aware of me. She came to the outside door with me and once again I promised that I would see that the army knew what was going on. As I walked up the road I turned and waved, she waved back and went indoors.

Battalion HQ, when I reached there, showed more activity than I had ever seen before. It was now a hive of activity with men rushing about everywhere. In the corner, two had started a fire and were feeding it from stacks of paper. My Company Sergeant Major had a little den where he conducted the never ending paper work of returns and orders. He was sitting at the table and I poked my head around the door: "Where the hell have you been?", he greeted me. I never gave a thought as to how he knew I was coming to HQ.

"Sir", I said, "Do you know there's a hospital full of Jerries just down the road and there are no guards?" "I don't know and what's more I don't bloody care", he said. "We're pulling out and nobody has time to bother about Jerries now". For a moment I thought he meant we were moving positions but then he gave me a written message. "Get straight down to the Company and give this to the second in charge and for God's sake don't lose it or let anyone see it."

I took the message and scooted, not pausing until I was well clear of HQ. When I read it I felt sick. It was a order for all Officers to report to Battalion HQ. We were evacuating the island that very night. I could hardly believe it. We had soundly thrashed the Germans, kept possession of the airfields and although we were short of food, supplies and ammunition we had seemed set to stay on the island.

The little news that filtered through from the

The Promise

other end of the island was not too good. The New Zealanders and Aussies were having difficulties but that's all we rank and file knew about the situation. I hurried back down the road passing the hospital which once more seemed dead and deserted.

That night we left for other countries and other campaigns. Over the years I have wondered about the girl. Did she get punished for bringing in a British Soldier? What became of her? Did she survive the War? What did she think of the promise I made and broke?

How it came about that someone ran a hospital for German wounded in the middle of British positions unknown to anybody but the few people inside is a mystery I will never solve."

**JOHN WYATT.
BRADFORD. W. YORKS.**

Change of Orders

"June 20th 1940, saw me standing on Lowestoft Railway Station with a group of local lads. We had been instructed by notice from National Services (Armed Forces Act 1939) to report to the Officer I/C 50th Battalion Royal Norfolk Regt. ITC Britannia Barracks, Norwich, Norfolk for Military Service; we were told to be there between 9am and 12noon.

On arrival at Thorpe Station, Norwich, we were met by an Army M.T. Driver. His name was Dick Sadd, the brother of Ginger Sadd who was the area champion welterweight boxer. Dick asked us if we were joining the Royal Norfolks. If we were, he went on, jump on to the truck. We all piled on not knowing what to expect. Ten minutes later we arrived at a building, which turned out to be Town Close School, Newmarket Road, not Britannia Barracks where we should have reported to.

We were told to de-bus and form up on the playground. After a brief talk by a Major Atkinson, we were told to go into the building which was to be our billet and home for some time to come. We were fourteen to a room; our bed was a base of straw, as was the pillow.

Next day we were paraded and made up into Platoons 13, 14, 15 and were from then on, to be known as 'C' Company 50th Batt. Holding Unit. I was in 13 Platoon. Our Sergeant, Sgt. Mahoney, said he was going to make soldiers out of us and that we were going to be the best Platoon of all.

Change of Orders

We were told that there were four other companies A, B, C and D. He told us sternly, that we wouldn't let him down.

Next day we received our uniforms and other pieces of kit. After weeks of drill, route marches, weapon training, and being called all the names under the sun, we finally became fully fledged recruits. Although billeted in Norwich, we were not allowed a pass to get home which was only twenty five miles away. After Church Parade on a Sunday, the rest of the day was ours. For the Norwich boys it was just the job, as they were on home ground.

As the weeks rolled on and passes were still unavailable, a couple of others and I decided that we would go home after Church Parade, even if only for a few hours. I wanted to see my wife as I had only married in January of that year. Not being far from the rail station at Whittlingham, we decided to use that, as Norwich Station would more than likely be full of Red Caps. We had a great day and returned without any trouble.

We were now fully trained and were to be known as the 9th Batt. Royal Norfolk Regt. We were fully armed and available to be sent to any part of the world as a fighting unit; but that was not to be. Our orders arrived and we were sent to a town called North Walsham, not too far from Norwich.

We didn't do much training in the open. I was sent on a two week snipers course with some of the others where I achieved good results. On returning to the unit, I was told that we were to move again to the coast to relieve the units of the 18th Division. They were going to a lying up area to prepare for embarkation to the Far East. This turned out to be ill-fated Singapore. Some of my mates had been drafted from 9th Batt. to the 4th, 5th, and 6th Royal Norfolk, who were part of the 18th Div.

We marched from North Walsham to the Coast. I forget how many miles it was. 9th Batt. Royal Norfolk's sea defence areas were from Wells in North Norfolk down to Sea Palling. We covered Cromer, Blackney, Sheringham, Mundersley, Trimingham, Hapisbury Baiton and BHQ at Holt. We patrolled from one company area to another. In Cromer, we manned a Pill box which had instruments inside which, at the pull of a lever, could blow a hole in the Pier if a Jerry tried to land on it. Another task was to put coils and coils of barbed wire on the scaffolding which had been erected by the RCOs to stop any German advance if they were lucky enough to land and get that far after dodging the mines.

After a good spell on the Coast, we were on the move again, this time to the South of England. We arrived at Winchester Barracks as part of the 47th London Div. (Bow Bells) Signals. We were considered a good Battalion and would be shipped abroad as a fighting Division after more intense training. A change of orders again put us on the

Isle of Wight. We landed at Ryde and were split up and sent to different locations. My Company 'C' was assigned to Sandown. By now we were filling drafts to reinforce other regiments and that ruled out any chance of us going out as a fighting unit. Our stay on the Island was pretty easy. We did the usual guard duties on Company and HQ billets.

After a while, we were on the move again, this time to Boscombe, Bournemouth. We hadn't much to do here; the usual guards, weapon training and not much else. By this time I had my first stripe and baptism under enemy fire. My brother and I, who had joined the Battalion at Winchester, were looking out to sea, when we saw three planes flying low approaching the town. On nearing the cliff one plane couldn't get the height. He crashed and exploded. The other two circled the town and dropped bombs.

Bournemouth was the rest area for Airmen who had done their share of missions. In the raid, hotels that housed these airmen were hit. There were many casualties. One hotel, The Metropole, took a direct hit. What a terrible sight it was. The whole gable end had been torn off and the bodies of airmen could be seen hanging from the ruins. We were told to keep moving as there were several other personnel helping to search through the bricks and debris for the bodies of the airmen.

We moved again. This time to Hambledon near Portsmouth. We were filling many drafts to other units still. After three years of travelling around with the 9th Norfolks my luck ran out. I was sent on draft leave with twenty of my comrades. My younger brother stayed with the unit but I found out later he was drafted to the 1st Batt. Royal Sussex Regt. He was then posted abroad.

My comrades and I returned from leave and were told that we were to join the 2nd Batt. Bedford, Hertfordshire Regt., wherever they were. We found ourselves at Southampton where we were put on a troop train. After twenty four hours travelling, we arrived at Liverpool. We walked from the station to the docks in the early hours of the morning carrying our kit bags and equipment. After the formalities were over, we boarded the troopship Franionia. She was already crowded with troops, and still we didn't know where we were going. We thought we were going to sail but it was not until the next night that we slipped out of Liverpool to join the convoy.

After two weeks at sea, without any interference from aircraft or submarines, we landed at Algiers, North Africa in December, 1943. After disembarkation, we marched to a place called Maison Corree and a very welcome meal. Later we were introduced to a Major Marlin who was to be my Company CO. He had a list of names who he had to form into Platoons. I remained in 13 Platoon 'C' Company. My Lowestoft pals Ted Baxter and Dennis Read were allocated to 'A' Company. The

Change of Orders

other Royal Norfolks who I came out with were allocated to other Companies.

Later on we learnt that the 2nd BN Bedfords, after fighting in France, were sent to North Africa to fight in the Desert Campaign where they sustained many casualties. Our draft along with others, were to be their replacements. I had to take down my stripe as they were up to strength with older members of the Battalion. After settling down in our new formation we moved to the desert where we lived in tents. We did a lot of training. The weather was very hot during the daytime but cold during the night.

Word was passed round that we were to leave Egypt but nobody knew where we were going. We were to leave all the equipment behind, even company weapons. Before long, we boarded a train at Port Said and headed for Tewfik for another sea trip. We embarked on a smaller trooper; it was a dirty ship that had been used for carrying Palestine's refugees. Rumour was going round that we were bound for England. Everyone seemed to think so. After a short journey, we steamed into what turned out to be the Port of Naples. Our role as a fighting unit was to be in Italy.

We were now a part of 10th Brigade, 4th British Division, 8th Army. We disembarked and moved into the suburbs of the City. We stood around talking for a while, not knowing what was in store for us. It wasn't long before we knew. A convoy of Army trucks drew up and we were hustled aboard and quickly moved off. We were on our way to the Front.

After miles of travelling we came to a halt and Companies were ushered into different groups. My Company under Major Martin was on its way. It wasn't long before we encountered mountain tracks. We finally reached our positions. The Mountain was called Cerosala. It had previously been occupied by the troops we had relieved. One or two graves covered with stones lay about. Our positions were called 'Sanyars' which were like birds' nests made of stone.

It was winter time by now and the battle Front was static. We were to be stuck here until the Spring offensive. The rest of the Battalion were scattered in positions on different mountains. Below Cerosala, ran a valley separating us from a mountain directly to our front. We could see soldiers moving about and we assumed they were one of our Companies. Each morning these self same soldiers could be seen shaking blankets. We used to wave and they waved back. This went on for some time until one day we were waving, when suddenly a mortar shell came over. Luckily it didn't cause any damage as we were on the right side of the slope. It appears that the soldiers who we were waving to were German. Apparently they had been relieved and the new arrivals did not take to kindly to our waving. We had to forget that for a while.

Change of Orders

The Spring Offensive was about to begin. I had gained my second stripe and we were going into action. I was instructed to go down the mountain to a lying up area and guide a Company of Guards up to our positions. We set off in good spirits and all went well for a while. We kept to the small tracks, puffing and blowing now and then, as it was up hill all the way. For some unearthly reason snow began to fall, not much to start with but soon it became heavy. Strange spring weather.

The light was fading fast and the snow was still falling. The whole area was covered in a white blanket. It was difficult to keep to the tracks; eventually it became hopeless. The lads were moaning and swearing. I remember thinking to myself this lot were going to murder me. We ambled on a few more steps slipping and sliding and not knowing where we would end up. After a stop or two to get directions, I thought we were lost. I wondered what kind of reception I would get when we did eventually get back. Or would we end up in the German positions?

It started to get light, the sky was blue, the snow was melting, we only had a few more yards to go and we were in the Company area. We handed over and nothing was said about us being late. 'C' Company moved down the mountain to join the Battalion. Each Company took up it's allocated Battle Positions, and the Spring Offensive for us, had begun.

The 8th Army, along with the American 5th Army, proceeded to battle it out together. Progress was slow as the Germans had had months and months to prepare their positions. Some very good natural defences. As the weather improved the Armies made considerable progress on all sectors, making the Germans fall back to other prepared positions.

Further progress of the Allied Advances had to come to a stop. Cassino, a market town defended heavily by the Germans and overlooked by Monti Cassino, was a very commanding observation post for the Germans. This was to cause headaches for the Allies. The American 5th Army tried unsuccessfully to take the town of Cassino and each time sustained many casualties. There were three attempts to dislodge the enemy, but each time they failed.

Now a fourth attempt was going to be made. My own Battalion, 2nd Beds. Herts. Regt. and the 4th British Division, were going to take part in the battle for Cassino. After a briefing in a backward area behind Mount Trocchio, the Battalion advanced to the Companies separate start lines before the River Rapido.

11th May, and it was dark now. The mines had been cleared and white tapes had been fixed so we could find our way to the River bank. My Company was allotted two boats to get across to the other side. We had been told that the river was fast flowing,

41

W A R · M E M O R I E S

Change of Orders

about 8 knots. About 23.00hrs, all hell let loose: 1400 guns opened fire on known enemy positions. It was time. Some of the boats were sunk as we crossed when the enemy spotted us. The boats which managed to cross safely returned for another load.

Across the other side, the Battalion ran into stiff opposition. They were not yet in their allotted positions. My Company ran into an A.P. minefield where we sustained many casualties. Sgt. Saunders and Prvt. Pierce, who were just ahead of me and others behind, were killed. It was awful. We lay there until daybreak not daring to move.

Capt. Taylor did a great job in finding a way through. He was awarded the MC. The Battalion was supposed to be on the final objective by 04.00hrs but owing to the difficulties encountered, we were not completely over the Rapido until 07.00hrs 12th May. We had no support weapons with us, and would not get any until the bridgehead was enlarged. Jerry knew this and was giving us a rough time with the mortars.

We were hoping for reinforcements but had to hold our own until this was possible. A bridge had to be built during the night. The Sappers started on it as we were being shelled and suffered many casualties. The night of the 13th we moved forward and made advances through the Gustav Line. On the 14th we were attacked again. During the long battle we again lost many men.

On the 16th May, we made it to Cassino; it had been a costly adventure.

The Battalion's strength initially was five hundred men. When relieved, we had lost half of that total. We had done our part.

After rest and reinforcement, Cassino was no more. We continued our role chasing Jerry and keeping him on the run. Our task in Italy finished on the outskirts of Florence. We were relieved by the 1st Armoured Division and came out of the line for a rest and left Italy for good.

My last and final move in the Army was to Greece, when the Battalion took part in the domestic trouble there. I was demobbed from Athens in March, 1946. I was part of 27 Group and sailed home to England.

I had served for three years with the Royal Norfolks and three years with the Bedford and Hertford Regt."

5778435
Ex Sgt. W. Pickers.
LOWESTOFT.
SUFFOLK.

The Longest Evacuation Line

Madras to Rangoon.

"We were back at Avadi Camp again. Avadi was about fifteen miles inland from Madras, only this time we were quarantined. We consisted of about eighty BORs and ten Officers of the RAMC draft RXKHX, who had all volunteered in August 1941, in response to a request for men who were single, medically A.1. and the ORs at least, nursing orderly class 2. This is a short history of four of that draft. John Luff of HQ Coy, Cyril Seaward of A. Coy, Ron Willenbruch of 129th Field Ambulance 43rd Div. and myself, Arthur Scott of B. Coy, 132nd Field Ambulance 44th Div.

We had embarked mid Feb., 1942 onto the troop ship S.S. Neuralia with the 1st Battalion the Cameronians at Madras. When at sea, two transports joined us. When we arrived at Rangoon, we discovered that the 7th Armoured Brigade had already started to disembark from them. The docks were deserted, no wharf labour in sight. We followed the Cameroonians off the ship, watched them embus onto trucks and vanish. We stood at ease for about two hours.

Two Military Police turned up in a truck and told us that all the wharf labour had fled from Rangoon with many of the Burmese people, due to the Japanese bombing. All military stores were being moved out and the oil terminal was ready to be destroyed. A staff car turned up and after a discussion with our senior Officer, we were told to re-embark, as all the wounded and sick troops in Rangoon, along with nursing sisters, would be evacuated to Madras and the first casualties were already on their way to the ship.

We spent several hours clearing the mess decks and carrying stretcher cases on board, organising the different decks for surgical, medical and VD cases, bedding them down on mattresses and organising ourselves into shifts and duties. We were feeding and treating several hundred BORs, Indian ORs, a few Burmese and some Officers. Being new to Indian troops, we knew nothing of the diet problems in feeding Hindus and Moslems. We were to have plenty of time during the next three years to overcome them.

When the nursing sisters came on board, they were completely exhausted after a day of supervising the evacuation of the hospitals. At least they had the Officers' Quarters to relax in as this was a troop ship. At dusk we left the docks heading for the open sea, but it was the next morning, with the ship vibrating on all deck levels that someone told us that we had no escort. Then it sunk in that if we hit trouble, many of the wounded were unable to wear life jackets and it was a long way to carry them to the boat deck.

Many of us slept the night on the mess decks

with the patients. It was then that we learned that we had small-pox patients on board. Though they were isolated with two of our orderlies, we knew we would all be quarantined when we landed. We arrived back at Madras and no one was allowed near the ship. We had to carry all the stretcher cases down to the wharf and on to the ambulances and supervise all walking patients onto the hospital train, making sure none of the VD cases tried to desert. They were in fact under arrest for being unfit for duty. VD was classified as self-inflicted during active service. That evening a special two carriage train took us back to Avadi for vaccinations and two weeks confined to camp.

MADRAS TO CHITTAGONG

As soon as the quarantine period ended, our wonderful run of luck started in that we four, whatever happened, always finished up back together again. Twenty four ORs (yes, we were in the party) twenty Privates, three Corporals and one Sergeant and no Officers!! We never saw any of our draft Officers again. We were given our movement orders and started a journey that would take us several thousand miles during the next three and a half years.

At Madras, we entrained and arrived in Calcutta and stayed at Dum Dum racecourse for two days, then started the journey that many thousands of troops bound for the Arakan, were to follow. From broad gauge train and ferry, down river, then on to the narrow gauge line, through Chandpur to Chittagong to meet a sight that was to become very familiar during our next few weeks in Burma. Thousands of Indian refugees were fleeing from south Burma walking across the ranges to the coast. We were then transported by boat up the coast to Chittagong.

Our Sergeant had plenty of paper and movement orders, because everything was going like clockwork - not at all like the Army! We were taken to the Chittagong Club (very posh) of all places. I wondered what the old timers would have said, our kit all over the place, being served drinks and waited on by the servants in the dining room. Then came the first surprise, an Officer gathered us together and told us we would be flying to a place called Shewbo in central Burma at 0800 hrs next morning. No kit bags to be taken, only packs and webbing. We would be flying in a DC3 Civil aircraft that was engaged in flying out civilian refugees from Shewbo, mostly women and children.

BURMA AND THE RETREAT

A flight was due soon, so we moved into the lounge to stay the night. The party arrived, most of the women were very distressed having left their husbands and other male relatives, their homes and possessions, not knowing if they would ever see them again. The Indian staff and the local British Club members were wonderful, coping with four plane loads each day.

Next morning we were transported to the local airfield where we boarded the plane. All the seats had been stripped out and continuous row of metal bucket seats were fixed to each side. We stacked all our kit on the floor down the middle, then we were off on our second journey to Burma. From the air the view was just endless miles of trees, we crossed a river (the Chindwin) and the country then opened up to dry paddy fields and irrigation canals. As we off-loaded from the plane at Shewbo, the next party of civilian refugees were waiting ready to board.

In the afternoon, we were taken to the station and onto a train to Mandalay. I will always remember crossing the Irrawaddy River on the Ava Bridge and admiring the wonderful engineering structure that was destined, just a few short weeks later, to be blasted into the river.

On arriving in Mandalay, we were taken to Fort Durrerin which we found out later had been a Palace of the King of Burma before British rule and most of the buildings were destroyed in the 1945 campaign. We were billeted in the Cantonment (barracks). Though nobody knew, or would tell us, where or to which unit we were to join, our transit

was amazing us all.

On the move again next day to Mandalay station, onto a train we were told to Lashio, the railhead near the Chinese border and the beginning of the Burma Road. Again we marvelled at the railway engineering of the zig-zag track up the face of the escarpment from the plains. The massive Goktiek Viaduct out of a tunnel, across the deep gorge and back into a tunnel again. At Lashio, we were transported to, of all places, an RAF camp and for our first time billeted in a bamboo basha (hut). We spent many months in 1943/44 working in those ingenious huts.

Now, our luck ran out. All that wonderful organisation ground to a halt, nobody knew what to do with us. After four days we were on the move again, this time, back down the line to Maymyo halfway between Lashio and Mandalay. On our way to Lashio we had passed several trains on the down track for Mandalay loaded with Chinese troops. Lashio was crowded with thousands of them.

We were loaded onto a Chinese troop train and our first close contact with Chiang Kai-Shek's Army. Now our journey became a farce. At one of the stations when the up train arrived, the second party of twenty four and the last from our draft at Madras, like us without any Officer, were willy-nilly going up to Lashio while we were on our way back.

When I look back and think of the cost and organisation during those desperate days of the

The Longest Evacuation Line

Burma Campaign, to move our party of forty eight ORs from Madras to the Chinese border, the project at some time in the past must have been top priority. On arriving at Maymyo, we were taken to the peace time barracks. Maymyo was a Government and Civil Service Hill Station with lavish homes and buildings still living a pre-war existence, soon to be rudely shaken to the fact that the Japs now had no opposition in the air. Two days later, our second group joined us.

It was now late March, 1942. Though we obviously were unaware at the time, Burma was already lost. After Rangoon fell, all reinforcements and supplies to Burma stopped. When the Chinese were defeated at Taoungoo on the main road and the railway from Rangoon to Mandalay, and the 17th Div. had to evacuate Prome on the Irrawaddy and the last of the RAF was bombed out of Magwee Airfield, the Japs could now bomb as and when they pleased, which they did with awesome results as we were to taste. Cyril and Ron at Maymyo, John at Lashio and myself at Meiktila and Shewbo.

They came over in gaggles of thirty or more unescorted, circled the town at least twice, closed up and let everything go together, crude but very effective. They had been doing it in China for years. You could see all the bombs leaving the planes, then there was one almighty bang, then they would serenely glide away, not an A.A. gun to salute them. At least it was quick. The local people who had survived just fled and left the buildings to burn; the whole Civil Services vanished.

Several of our party (Cyril, Ron and John) had been drafted to the Burma General Hospital, others to the Indian General Hospital, both functioning in Maymyo, and ten of us were ordered to go down to Yenangyaung in the oilfields area near the Irrawaddy to bring back casualties.

That morning, we were ordered to parade and an Officer introduced himself. Major Calvert from the Bush Warfare School. He told us that our draft was to have been part of the columns that the school was to have trained for long range penetration work. We were then told that all the men not under orders were to collect their kit and board the trucks waiting outside. That was about twenty of our forty eight.

When our group was en-route to Yenangaung, first joining our trucks in Mandalay, we found the city a shambles. It had been bombed twice, the centre was burnt out and deserted. There was no shortage of trucks, all American, part of the supplies meant for the Burma Road and China. When we arrived at Yenangyaung, we found that the 17th Div. and the Chinese were preparing to defend the oilfields. We were ordered to load as many casualties as possible and with one orderly to each of the ten trucks, we headed north for Meiktila.

We stopped at an ordnance unit near a railway siding just outside the town to feed and attend to

The Longest Evacuation Line

the casualties. We had a grandstand view of the bombing of the town. Down came the bombs in one great swish and bang, the closest a few hundred yards away. It was all over so quickly, we had no chance to lift down the stretcher cases from the floor of the trucks. Everyone just sat and hoped.

Before we left in a convoy for Maymyo, the Sergeant in charge of transport called us orderlies together to warn us about the Chinese transport using the road that wound down from Maymyo to Mandalay. He told us to stand looking out over the driver's cabin and if we heard any vehicle coming down the road, to bang on the cabin roof to give the driver a chance to find a spot to pull well over, as the Chinese driving standards were awful and many head-on collisions had occurred.

Both the Burma and Indian General Hospitals were preparing for evacuation when we handed over the casualties on our return to Maymyo. I was now attached to the Indian Hospital, it was mid April and we spent several days making plaster bandages and immobilising the limbs of all the arm and leg casualties.

While I was down south, Cyril and Ron at the Burma Hospital were having a hectic time. When Maymyo was bombed, four bombs fell in the compound killing several people. The staff there were also plastering all the limb cases and getting ready for evacuation.

John was having more than his fair share of adventure. He was sent to Lashio with a truck load of medical supplies whilst all the patients from both hospitals were loaded onto the trains waiting at a well sheltered siding outside Maymyo. Both hospitals closed down and the trains at night went down the escarpment and over the Irrawaddy on the Ava Bridge, heading north for Myitkyina.

Maymyo was crowded with Chinese stragglers, many of them wounded. Medical services for the Chinese were non-existent. All of the troops were trying to get onto trains and trucks heading for Lashio and China. Two surgeons and a few of us BORs and IORs stayed behind and set up a surgical team. Throughout the war I never again saw such awful casualties. Nearly half were gangrenous. We only had one steriliser for the instruments and we set up two operating tables. We used pentothal for the first anaesthetic and then dripped chloroform from the bottle on to a face mask. At the end of the day, we all had wonderful headaches. A few Chinese orderlies stayed with the amputees, but I don't think many of the poor devils would have survived as by now, the Japs had cut road and rail links with Lashio.

When we left Maymyo heading for Mandalay and the bridge across the Irrawaddy, the town seemed deserted. I understand that two spans of the bridge were blown the following afternoon. We reported to the last large medical unit still working outside Shewbo. It was near a railway siding as all

47

The Longest Evacuation Line

the units still in the area were moving off to the Chidwin at Kalewa and Pantha for the march out to India. Any casualties and sick were left at Shewbo. Again the place was crowded with Chinese troops trying to organise rail transport to Myitkyina. They were trying to commandeer anything they could get their hands on. They'd had plenty of practice having lived off the land, fighting the Japs in China since the early 1930s.

Our people had assembled a train from a few old carriages and goods wagons. This was heavily guarded night and day by troops to keep the marauding Chinese away. I must repeat, that it was many months later that we learned and realised the gravity of the events happening around us and how vital was the timing of the retreat to Imphal and the Irrawaddy, to Myitkyina and the Hukawng Valley.

The medical personnel spent nearly a day moving all the patients to the train doing everything possible to make them comfortable in the harsh, hot conditions. The worst cases were placed on the seats of the carriages, but getting from compartment to compartment to feed and supply drinks and tend to dressings and medication, was only possible with stops at every siding platform along the way.

A few nurses and sisters, Burmese, Indian and British, the MOs, Indian cooks and orderlies all worked with great devotion and discipline. At Naba Junction that night we witnessed a tragedy that

even the greatest fiction writer could not have bettered.

As the army had retreated northwards through central Burma, nearly all the railway rolling stock had been concentrated on the Mandalay-Lashio section or on the single track from Shewbo to Myitkyina. Many of the staff had opted to stay in their own regions, so only the British Anglo-Indian and Anglo-Burmese staff whose families had been air evacuated to India remained. They had been given military rank.

I have never read of any official recognition of the wonderful work they did, keeping the line open and somehow resisting, the sometimes armed pressure of the would be Chinese hijackers. The staff had problems ensuring that the four trains carrying the casualties arrived at Myitkyian on separate days, so as not to cause bottlenecks or targets for any Jap bombing raids on the airfield. This placed extra strain on the nursing staff as it had been decided that only the nurses and sisters and a few MOs from each train, would go into Myitkyina and to the airfield and so care for the casualties on the flights to India.

Our train was halted alongside the platform of the Naba Junction, so easing our job of feeding all the men. Most of the sidings were full of wagons, many containing Chinese squatters. The major cause of the following tragedy was the breakdown of the pump to the overhead water tank which supplied water to the engine tenders.

Early the following morning a very long train, packed with Chinese troops and stores (an official train) pulled out heading north up the so called Railway Corridor. They were bound for Mogaung and the trek up the infamous Hukawng Valley to Ledo. From Naba to Malwu was a very steep gradient along which, at a bridge, a watering point had been set up. As we found out later that day, dozens of four gallon cans were provided and a chain gang was formed to pass up the cans from the Chaung (creek) to the tender. This took about two hours when we did it.

This procedure must have happened to the troop train and it was assumed that with the length and weight of the train and maybe lack of experience of the driver and fireman, they could not achieve traction when trying to restart the train and perhaps, added to by the exasperated Chinese Officer who told them to unhitch some of the wagons. This was done.

At Naba Junction, our first realisation of anything amiss, was the shrill squealing of the wagon wheels on the track rushing towards us. One of the railway staff must have been quickly aware of the danger as we found out later that he had switched the points to the track furthest from the platform. With an astounding crash that seemed to last for minutes, the wagons piled into the stationary line of trucks. When the dust cleared and we had rushed over, the unbelievable pile, over twenty feet high, of smashed woodwork, wheels and metal frames stopped us short. Nobody spoke, then we heard the moans under the heap.

The impact must have been awesome. Before we could get ourselves organised, the Chinese surrounded the area with armed troops and our MOs told us to leave as they did not want to provoke an incident with the very edgy Chinese who were looking for someone to blame.

The date was the 1st May and while we had spent forty eight hours at Naba Junction, Cyril's and Ron's train had arrived at Mogaung, about twenty miles from Myitkyina where they were told about the evacuation details. They would return down the line (just the personnel of the Burma Hospital without the nurses) to Hopin and prepare for a march out to India.

John was having his problems with the Chinese. After a few days at Lashio working in the railway hospital with the Japs on the outskirts of the town, a convoy of six trucks with mostly wounded Chinese left for Namtu with John and another orderly in charge. As John said 'in charge' was definitely not the operational word with a total language barrier. The Chinese drivers were heading for Namkham and the Chinese border. But luckily, they were turned back and after six days and several hundred miles, they hit the Irrawaddy and somehow got a boat up to Katha and onto the last Hospital train.

The Longest Evacuation Line

Later, on May 2nd, after I had got off our train on seeing Cyril, John turned up, so the four of us were together again after moving over most of north Burma; luck had united us for our long walk.

THE MARCH OUT TO INDIA

Again I must stress, though we were ignorant of the overall picture of events that were engulfing us, luck was surely on our side. First I am sure our survival as a party of nearly one hundred non-combatants of mixed races with no experience or training for jungle marching, no equipment and very scanty rations (mostly rice) we few BORs having only been in Burma a few weeks, completely un-acclimatised and very basically clad, was due to two men. Number one was the senior MO of the Burma prisons, Major Raymond; the second a person we never got to know except that he was in his fifties and must have been a District Officer in northern Burma of many years standing, well-liked and respected by all the local Burmese.

He had a few years previously, walked the tracks we were to take, on a previous holiday in Imphal, duck shooting. Apparently the Imphal Plains were famous in peacetime as a shooter's dream, which when one thinks of what was to happen within two years, is very ironic. We rarely saw him, as he was always a day's march ahead of us, organising the local village leaders to help feed us. This in itself must have been a strain supplying a meal for nearly one hundred people consisting of approx. ten Officers, eight BORs, twenty Anglo Indian and Anglo Burmese orderlies, sixty Indian orderlies, cooks, water carriers, sweepers and batmen (very few Burmese).

Our route out had not been used by the thousands of Indian refugees that had fled from the Burmese more than the Japs. They had gone over the ranges to the coast, up the Chindwin to Imphal and the worst trek from Mogaung up the Hukawng Valley to Ledo, leaving a trail of death and disease - cholera, dysentery and small-pox through which Bill Slim's Army had to retreat to Imphal and the Chinese to Ledo.

We were divided into sections of about twenty, with two MOs per section. Our section consisted of the BORs and the Anglo Indian-Burmese. We all started with a full pack. One blanket, mosquito net, change of underclothing, two pairs of socks, mess tin, water bottle and a couple of tins of bully beef or milk.

We were soon to see the discipline that Major Raymond intended to enforce and which no doubt helped to save our lives. The local headman had complained that two IORs had broken into one of the village huts. The Major had us all assembled to witness them getting ten strokes each of a lash delivered by a Havildar.

The Longest Evacuation Line

The Major then told everyone that looting or interfering with the local women would alienate the people, who would then not assist us with food or shelter. Don't forget, we only had about six rifles to protect ourselves with. During the next nineteen days and three hundred miles, the water, hygiene and general discipline was exemplary. Cyril kept a diary which is referred to here.

The first day, May 4th, was a shake down day. We only marched eight miles, but soon settled down to a well organised routine. We had six bullocks with panniers to carry the dixies and some tinned rations. A different section led the column each day. We marched the usual fifty minutes then had a ten minute break. We had an early start about 0600hrs after a meal of cold rice and vegetables and a cup of tea (black) from the previous night's cooking.

Cyril noted that we marched through a heavy rain storm on the second day. We were told it was part of the Chota Monsoon or pre monsoon rains of which we were to live through almost four, before we left Rangoon in late 1945.

We marched for eight days, staying in a village most nights and being made most welcome by the headman and villagers. We now know this was entirely due to the goodwill and regard the local people had towards our District Officer.

We had marched around the fresh water lake called Indawgyi and on the eighth evening, reached the River Uyu. The next five days were to be a unique experience. From Cyril's diary :-

Day 7, May 10th, miles 16, total 95.

Started to march at 7am and had a terrible day, the track was very rough and hilly and soon tired us out. After 16 miles, came to a village on the bank of quite a large river called the Uyu. The village was having a festival, the villagers brought us out some sweetmeats, mostly popcorn in toffee and ginger and little pancakes; after a rest and a bathe in the river, the villagers cooked us a meal of curried vegetables and rice and we all enjoyed it! We were lucky enough to be invited to a Pongyi Festival, where four boys were being initiated as Pongyis, (Buddhist Priests) After more sweetmeats, they took offerings to the temple and we witnessed native dancing. After practice loading of the boats, we found sleep nearly impossible because of the swarms of sandflies.

Day 8, May 10th, first day on river, miles 20, total 115.

Rose very early and had usual cold breakfast. Carried our kit to the boats, loaded kit and ourselves and 7am saw us on our way. The boat we were in was a 24 foot long tree trunk hollowed out with bamboo outriggers and bamboo and banana leaf shades and it held eight of us and two river men. All the boat people had blue intricate tattooing from hip to ankle all over both legs. Although we only had sign language, they were wonderfully cheerful people. We had walked for two days parallel with the river, now we understood why.

The river was very shallow and we often had to get into the water and push the boat off the sand banks, we also had to paddle and row ourselves and caused much amusement to the boat men who though happy, were lazy. Thinking about this later, I realised that they knew they would have to work the boat back up river against the current and the monsoon was due to break any day.

Day 11, May 14th, miles 19, total 174.

Rose at 4.40am and dressed. That is, I put on my shirt and packed my blanket and went to get breakfast. As usual it was cold cooked rice; and a little veg. Drew rations for the day's journey which was stewed pork and rice, didn't fancy the pork so just had the rice. Stopped at a village along the river and collected some more raw rice as we only had four day's supply left and we were told we have at least another eight days marching when we land

on the west bank of the Chindwin River below Homalin. The two boat men are rowing now and seem very happy singing their songs all day but we think they would like to get rid of us and head for home. We were getting too close to the Japs! Anyway, they ought to be happy as it's the first work they have done today and it's 4.20pm.

Four aircraft passed over, so we all pulled to the trees on the bank. They returned about an hour later. We passed a raft with an MO and three patients. We couldn't give him any help as we had no equipment, only field dressings. We soon left them behind as we were travelling very steadily. A message was relayed from boat to boat, no water to be used for food or drinking from now on unless boiled for five minutes as we were entering the area where cholera was prevalent.

It was 7.45pm when we disembarked. A storm was brewing from the west and as we were given our billet in a temple compound the storm broke. I had never seen it rain so hard, nor so much lightning and thunder. We had just had some tea from the Pongyi and it was jolly good! A crowd of us sat in a half circle around a fire and he dished out tea in little bowls and I was given a native cheroot (first smoke in nearly two weeks.) We were all bare footed in the temple.

I'm starving as I've only had a little to eat today - cold rice and two bananas. We have just received a present from the villagers, some crystallised ginger, cane sugar and honey, with of all things, potatoes for the morning.

Day 13, May 16th, miles 20, total 218.

Last day on the river, many happenings today. Entered the Chindwin with Homalin on the west bank. We didn't see the place really, only a small village. Pulled into the east bank again as a plane (could have been a DC3) was circling around very low to the south of us. Capt. Macdonald, who was our section Officer and rode in our boat, suggested the plane might be dropping supplies which gave us something to talk about as most of our conversation these days was around the topic of food. We all carried about seven pounds of rice each. I had mine wrapped in my spare shirt.

So it was rice every day, plus any fruit or vegetables we could buy from the villagers, which was usually not much when shared between nearly one hundred people. We had a very long day rowing, as we were making for a place called Tonhe, on the west bank where we would start marching again. We could see the huge range of hills that we would have to climb, over 4,000 feet high and we were told, fifty miles as the crow flies, but more than double the distance following the track. As the monsoon had started and we were getting heavier

and longer rains each day, we might have to take a two day detour to find a footbridge to cross a river called Yu, which could now be in spate.

We arrived at Tonhe just before dark and had an emotional farewell with our wonderful happy boat people, who had earned every rupee they had been paid. After the way the people in central Burma had reacted to the army, often waylaying and murdering stragglers, when they realised that the Japs were taking over Burma, we all knew, (at least the Officers and BORs) that but their loyalty to the District Officer, they could have abandoned us any night and left us stranded on the east bank of the river as each day we had progressed south and nearer to the Japs coming up the river.

That evening, while we were cooking our rice and boiling water for our bottles, we had another encounter, this time with some Royal Marines of all people, who had come up river in a large launch guarding the imprest of the army that had been marching up from the south towards Imphal, and surprise, having been told we would be marching through the edge the Naga Country, going westwards along tracks that had been soiled by the fleeing Indian refugees.

The Nagas would only trade for silver Rupees, (no paper money) so we were all given ten each. The story that was passed around was that the marines were going to sink the launch, money and all, in the middle of the Chindwin. I often wondered if they all got out to Imphal OK.

We soon got organised into our marching sections again for the early start next day. We had a long bamboo for carrying our two Dixies. We now had just a little salt, no tinned food or milk but plenty of rice. Each evening we put a tin mug full of rice from our packs into the dixie and any vegetables we had managed to buy and taking turns, four of us would scrounge around for enough wood and bamboo to start the fires going. One for the food and one for the drinking water.

I think we were always amazed, that with such an odds and sods crowd of people, the standards of discipline, hygiene and water discipline was maintained at such a high level throughout the nineteen days and three hundred miles. On the march, the bamboo pole with the dixies was passed down the line shouldered by two men for about twenty minutes.

We had a few sick, but we didn't lose a man. John Luff was our only unlucky marcher in our section. He must have contracted Malaria during his trek with the Chinese from Lashio to the Irrawaddy as he had two very bad days during our last week to Imphal. Though we did not actually carry him, we supported him for miles and made him stay on his feet, even when we took our ten minute break.

The last four days, as we were always soaking wet and cold, we just kept going. We soon started to shiver if we stopped so we just slogged on. The night after we crossed the River Yu, we just laid in the track as we stopped in our sections and went to sleep in the mud and rain.

Day 14, May 17th, miles covered 12, total 230. Tonhe to Thanan.

Rose at 4am. Breakfast was cold rice, no tea! Started at 5am. Found the track very rough, many trees felled across the track. It got harder and harder and very steep. In all we climbed about 1,400 feet in three hours and sweated almost away. I felt very weak and tired, mainly because we had been sitting very cramped in the boat for so many days and we hadn't had much leg exercise.

Day 15, May 18th, miles 15, total 245. Thanan to River Yu.

Reveille at 4am. Breakfast at 5am, just the usual rice and cha. Moved off at 5.30am, still dark. Covered about six miles by 8am, then came the 'HILL'. It was the hardest hill I'd ever climbed, the track went straight up and was very rocky. We climbed to 3,500 ft, according to the map, then on to a village about three miles away. After a further mile, much shouting from the sections behind, "Clear the track! Clear the track!" Charging along came about twenty armed Chinese, about ten very smart Frontier Force troopers with horses and pack mules, five white Officers and about ten Burmese nurses.

After they had vanished, Capt. MacDonald said it was the American General Stillwell and an American Doctor Seagrave with some of the Shan Hills Tribe Girls. No wonder they walked past us so briskly, they must have thought we were a real rabble. Capt. Mac. said that the plane that we saw two days ago must have been dropping them supplies before they crossed the Chindwin, maybe a rubber boat too.

Today we saw and smelled the first dead bodies alongside the track and banks of the River Yu, which we crossed by a well built footbridge. Now our water discipline will have to be very strict as water sources will all be fouled with human excreta. We passed a pile of bodies laid out five by five, stacked like kindling logs ready to be burned, so there must be some organisation around. We have noticed a big improvement in the track and guess we have crossed the border into India.

Day 16, May 19th, miles covered 10, total 273. Yu River to Sarbung.

As usual, cold rice and some black tea for breakfast. A very strong lecture on the water situation. Cholera is evident everywhere; we don't seem to notice being soaking wet all the time, just plod on and on. Spent the night at Sarbung, a Naga village. We bought a pig with our Rupees which took a very long time to cook - can't find dry wood anywhere these days.

Day 17, May 20th, miles covered 17, total 273. Sarbung to Manwunyang.

Up at 4.30am. Breakfast at 5.15am which was cold pork and rice. Again it was raining, so we kept going; soaked, cold and miserable. One good thing, the track was level, though boot deep with mud. But a long climb to the top, a steep descent and up and over again. We found the descents harder on the leg muscles - did the march non-stop as nobody wanted to stand around in the rain.

Day 18, May 21st, miles 12, total 285. Manwunyang to Kelihao.

Late start today. 6am rise, no breakfast, only tea. Marched off at 7am. Again a wet start, but the last hour we saw the sun and when we arrived at a camp, we were dry, the first time for days. The sun must have been a good omen, because we were told there was a supply depot. Loud

The Longest Evacuation Line

cheers!!! Our cooks of the day drew our rations, what riches. Tinned sausages, flour, sugar, porridge and powdered milk. We had a jolly fine meal of porridge, pancakes and tea, after which I went to sleep. Tomorrow we hear, will be our last day's march as we will reach the motor track and should pick up transport to a camp north of Imphal, so maybe we will sleep on a bed tomorrow. I didn't sleep at all during the night as the hut we occupied was lousy. I was bitten all over.

Day 19, May 22nd, miles 16 march. Truck 30. Keihao to Yaripok and Imphal.

We started off this morning with light hearts, as it was to be the last day of our ordeal. 6.30am saw us off and the first part was down a very steep decline for four miles. When we finished the down hill part it started to rain and soon we were drenched and very cold. We didn't stop and soon arrived at a small village after approx. 12 miles.

The locals sold us cooked rice, small cheroots, bananas and sweetmeats. Also cigarettes. We were directed to two large dry bamboo buildings and issued with more rations: sausages, (tinned) bully beef, sweetened rice and lovely hot sweet tea. Then I had a nap for an hour.

At 3pm, we started off to march to the road head where we were to pick up transport to the camp. It was raining as usual, so two soakings in the one day. I feel I have a cold coming on. (It was malaria).

We soon picked up transport which took us to Imphal. Yes we are back in the army. We had to change trucks which then took us to the camp. In my opinion it's a mud heap and very filthy. The huts are a very poor affair, made of bamboo and grass with mud floors covered with wet grass. We were very wet and after a meal, were issued with new clothes.

Day 20, May 23rd.

I woke up early, 5am. I think it was a force of habit. Breakfast was at 7.30 am, wonderful that someone else had prepared it: porridge, bully beef, bread and butter and very sweet tea. We gave our names to the orderly room and bought some cigs in the canteen. End of Cyril's diary.

Then came for us two days of horror and despair. I suppose one can understand our being kept well away from the fresh troops rushed up from India. They had little or no training and India Command still could not understand how the Japs so easily could overcome the under strength and under armed force that Bill Slim had held together and extracted from certain defeat.

So they decided it must have been the men and no way should the new troops be infected by lack of morale, and because the Indian refugees brought the plague of cholera, smallpox and dysentery with them, then so would the army, so they must all be quarantined.

This was to result in untold deaths. I'm sure no one ever found out how many of the retreating army died before or after eventually reaching Indian hospitals. I can however cite how our party were treated.

The next day, May 24th, we were moved from the camp and 'dumped' is the only word that can describe our treatment. Us few BORs with the Anglo Indian-Burmese and the Indian ORs, were trucked to a foul site (by now a rushing torrent.) This area must have held the surviving Indian refugees over the preceding weeks. The whole area down to the water's edge was fouled with human excreta. Some of it was the frightening sight of cholera stools. There were just a few shelters of bamboo and grass.

We were appalled at the complete breakdown of morale and discipline of the Indian troops and some of the Anglo boys. They just squatted in the filth and rain and would do nothing. We only ever saw one of the Officers again. That afternoon, Capt. MacDonald, nearly crying when he saw us, said:

"They said that we were a bloody nuisance." But fate was not to desert us. The second day, we were visited by an Indian MO.

He told us he was from a unit which had been in the van of Slim's retreat and most of his personnel had got through in good shape. It was the 8th Indian Casualty Clearing Station. Of course, they had no equipment but had been ordered to set up in the bombed civil hospital compound in Imphal.

They would have to look after BORs as well as Indian troops, they wanted BOR orderlies, would we help? He looked around and said: "You can't stay here can you?" Never did six men say: "Yes Sir!" with so much enthusiasm.

During the next three years, we often discussed the march and how fate looked after us and we often wondered if Major Raymond and the District Officer received any recognition of awards for bringing us through those nineteen days. We feel sure that they would not have voluntarily left us in such pitiful conditions."

**MR. A.G. SCOTT MR. C. SEAWARD.
UNIT 15/624 BRIDGE ROAD
SALISBURY EAST
SOUTH AUSTRALIA 5109**

The Artful Dodgers Of The Burma Road

- 1942

"Maymyo is a small town three thousand feet above the level of Mandalay in Burma. The solitary British military hospital had ran out of supplies and the Japanese Army was crushing the small opposition of British Empire Troops defending there.

Our 303 rifles and Bren guns were totally ineffective against an enemy that outnumbered us by thirty to one. We badly needed air support, tanks and big guns.

Evacuation of the hospital took days until all the patients were finally aboard the train. There were delays as it made its way north west. Saboteurs had blocked the railway lines by one means or another. Mandalay station had been bombed and the dead bodies were being eaten by wild dogs.

The Burmese Army had changed sides, walking over to join the Japanese to fight against us. Brainwashed by the enemy and with the promise of wresting the countries from the rule of the British, they were easy targets for Jap propaganda. The British were hated by the Burmese and I suppose they had reason to be. Whether freedom enriched their lives is a tale to tell later.

We arrived up in the hills heading for a place called Myitkyna. Along the way, the train pulled into a small roadside railway station where we could buy tea and curried vegetables sold from a small hand cart. I had tried to eat on a couple of occasions but could not hold any down. I was suffering with

CHAPTER 5

The Artful Dodgers Of The Burma Road

*Rangoon main
street peace keeping
picket during the
riots between the
Indian residents
there and the
Burmese.*

stomach ulcers at the time. I also had a suspected broken foot and my leg was in plaster from my toe to just below my knee.

We arrived at Myitkyna about midday where there was a meal of cooked rice waiting for us. In one of the lush green fields was a clapped out Blenheim Bomber.

The fields were marked off in oblong shapes surrounded by bunds. The bunds were made of heaped earth and they were adequate enough to withstand being filled with ankle deep water, thus enabling the rice seed sprouts to be planted.

Usually, in the hills, the temperature batted around eighty degrees for eighty percent of the year. In the autumn, the monsoons would come sweeping over the whole country flooding the land

The Artful Dodgers Of The Burma Road

filling the paddy fields for the rice planters.

There were a few bamboo shacks available for some of the patients. The rest of us had to sleep outside in the unbearable heat of the day.

The following day, we were gathered together and told there would be no more flights from Myitkyna. The Prime Minister had closed the Burma road to appease the Japs, thus depriving Shai Khan

Shek, the Chinese leader, of the vital supplies that were shipped by plane from Calcutta and along the Burma road by convoy. Except for a long trek over the hills, we were trapped.

The road was precarious as it was cut out of the hill sides and snaked for miles from China into Burma.

In the stifling heat of the afternoon, the silence

The Artful Dodgers Of The Burma Road

On guard duty - Maymyo. The Barrack rooms were made of wood and built on stilts to avoid flooding during the monsoons

before the impending floods came to drown them.

Suddenly, we were in semi-darkness. Heavy clouds swept towards us blotting out the sun. The air became cooler but a tornado-like wind tore at my clothes. I had been under many monsoons having spent six and a half years in Burma but in those, I could take shelter in the barracks. I struggled over to an upturned bullock cart and took my place beside a stranger. We held on tightly. Fork lightning lit up the sky, zig-zagging earthwards. The thunder was deafening.

I remembered a time in earlier years, when after the monsoon had passed, seeing a bullock turned to cinder after being struck by lightning. It was still standing.

Lightning was streaking all over the sky followed by thunderous crashes. The heavens opened up and glory be; rain, cold sweet rain. Buckets of it.

I was hanging on the wheel of the bullock cart as the wind kept trying to prise me loose. It may have lasted ten to fifteen minutes but it did subside and I was able to look skywards. I caught the falling rain in my mouth and like it or not I was getting a good shower.

As the clouds broke up, I could hear the thunder and see the lightning in the distance as the destroyer moved away. But for now, the rain kept on incessantly. Gradually the clouds uncovered the sun and the rain ceased leaving the paddy fields flooded.

was eerie. It seemed as though the wild life had gone into hiding, for not even a chirping bird could be heard. From out of the holes in the earth, hatched flying ants were escaping to a safe shelter

The Artful Dodgers Of The Burma Road

It was cooler and the birds were back. I looked around at the devastation, not a bamboo shack was upright. Some people had been lifted off their feet and blown away some distance. The Blenheim Bomber had been lifted into another field but now something else was happening to me. I knew what it was and found a nurse quickly. My malaria was back. I was developing a riga. My whole body shook. I felt frozen.

I was wrapped in blankets and given quinine tablets. I sweated profusely and was delirious. I had had these attacks several times but within half an hour I was back on my feet. I felt drained and the taste malaria left in my mouth was horrible.

We all heard it together, a loud noise and we all looked skywards. A solitary aeroplane circled above us. It landed and the pilot got out. A few of us approached him. He looked at us and said: "Goddamit! I took a beating up there in that storm. I had to land and spotted this field. I had no idea that there was anybody down here."

He turned out to be an American A.V.G. pilot, a voluntary group of pilots that were shuttling back and forth from Calcutta to China. This was to be his last trip before making his way home. He passed around the cigarettes whilst telling the Officer in charge that he would fly back to Calcutta over the Naga Hills to notify the RAF of our whereabouts. He would escort them here as long as they made their own way back. This would prove to be a dangerous task as the planes weren't fitted with the instruments to help them over the hills.

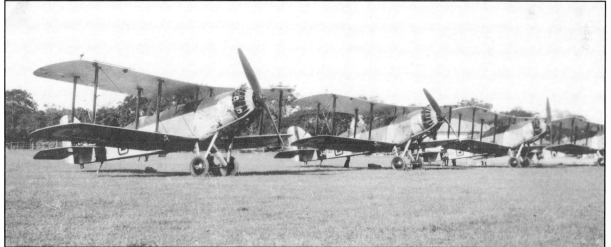

British airplanes, Mingladon, 13 miles from Rangoon. They disappeared after the fall of Singapore.

The Artful Dodgers Of The Burma Road

Burma Chinese border guard on Burma Road

Sometime later we spotted them and one by one they landed. It was decided that the civilians would fly out on the first plane, then the wounded on the second and so on. We were told to discard any surplus items in order to get as many on the planes as possible. I discarded my only boot, along with a few others. Ironically, I watched a soldier get into the plane carrying a portable gramophone and records. This could only have been looted. The soldier was off the convoy that was turned back when Singapore fell. He looked fit and active enough.

Whilst I waited to board the plane, I noticed the name on the side - 'Pan American Airlines'. It seemed shoddily built to me as the panels were held together with tiny rivets. I wondered just how the thing managed to fly. I climbed inside what was basically a hollow shell. All the seats had been stripped out in order to carry freight. We sat on the metal floor, packed in like sardines and took off.

I saw very little of the hills but I will never forget the air pockets. We dropped like a stone as the propellers grasped for air that wasn't there. No sooner had we got our stomachs back, when we'd hit another pocket. I decided there and then that I would never fly again. However, even though I was terrified at the time, I was certainly grateful to the RAF for saving my life.

We landed without a hitch in Assam. One of the worlds largest tea plantations. Women waited as we disembarked handing out tea and biscuits to us all. Imagine that. The first in weeks. I didn't have any problems keeping that down.

The following day, we were put on a train and we were finally taken to hospital. After being cleaned

The Artful Dodgers Of The Burma Road

up and my plaster removed, I was examined and put to bed. The staff were a recent contingent to the hospital and one nurse greeted me with the words: "The people back in England, don't think much of you lot in Burma. You let the British Army down".

Well, I couldn't argue with the nurse. After all, she was an Officer and I was only a corporal. In any case, we were warned to keep our mouths shut because if we had spoken out, it could have had a demoralising effect on our front line troops.

We couldn't tell them that the Nips were fanatics, all too eager to die in battle. We couldn't tell them we were vastly outnumbered and were fighting with sticks and bladders in a different kind of war. Years of field tactics and trench warfare had gone down the tube. This was jungle warfare. A War where a Jap would lash himself and a bag of rice up a tree and stay there sniping, ready to die if spotted. The British Army believes there is no finer fighting man than the Gurkha but a Japanese religious war fanatic took some beating.

Later perhaps, that young nurse would realise what it was all about. A big force of troops lined the Burmese-Indian border and one night, the Allies' tents were swarming with Japs. We had the numbers then, but this was a new type of warfare. There was so much chaos and death. I believe the divisional Commander got a roasting over that.

I often wonder what happened to my American A.V.G. Pilot. He deserved a medal as big as a frying pan for saving so many lives. Alas, not all the refugees made it though. Apparently the Japs got wind of the airlift and they managed to shoot down a few of the planes. My thanks to the RAF."

An extract from the 'Artful Dodgers on the Burma Road' by Ex Infantry Pioneer Sergeant 2nd Battalion of the King's Own Yorkshire Light Infantry, Mr. W. Robinson.

Chindits

Our thoughts are with you in this fateful hour. Victory where you are may mean ultimate victory in the Middle East. There will be no surrender and no evacuation.
Winston Churchill

"These words are etched onto my mind from May 1941. They were an order of the day sent to be read to us while we were trapped in Crete a few days after the German parachutists landed in the area. We were guarding the capital. The losses in ships, men and material during that battle were immense.

I was in the 2nd Battalion the Leicestershire Regiment. I joined them at Jericho, Palestine Feb, 1940, and we then left for Egypt and the Western Desert in Sept. of that year.

We left our base at Sidi Hanish to go on what was supposed to be a training operation. Monday Dec. 9th, we were called together, and our Officer spoke to us. He told us that we were actually going to attack the Italians the following day. "Anyone who is seen to turn and run will be shot. I shall personally shoot him myself," he said. I had reason to bear those words in mind.

The next day, at the height of the battle, I crawled many yards to a wounded man. He had a cap comforter over the right cheek of his behind. I looked at it and tried to comfort him. I had no water and neither had he. I asked him if he would like a drink as I had noticed a haversack several yards in front of us. I crawled over to it. It was empty. I had to shout back to him: "I'm sorry, I daren't come back to you. The stretcher bearers will be along in a minute." I just wasn't prepared to take the chance of turning my back on the Ities. I don't know if that chap made it. I never saw him again.

In Feb. 1941, we went back to Egypt. At one time in April we actually got to the stage of getting into the landing craft as it was rumoured that we were going to invade Rhodes Island. The next few days were really hectic. Back to the desert to Sidi Hanish, where I managed to retrieve a photo which I had put on a ledge in our old dugout that we had left six months earlier. It was a photo of my girlfriend. I had wrapped it in a leaf out of a Bible.

We were only there about a week, then back down to Alex onboard the ships 'Figi' and 'Gloucester.' We arrived on the night of Thursday, 15/16 May in Crete. Unfortunately both of these ships were sunk within a few days.

Hours later, Hitler sent an ultimatum to the Cretians. Surrender all British Troops on the island or else. These demands were dropped from the air in the form of leaflets.

They must have told him what to do with his leaflets, as the next day he sent about sixty bombers. They bombed the capital from the docks right through the town. From where I

66
W A R · M E M O R I E S

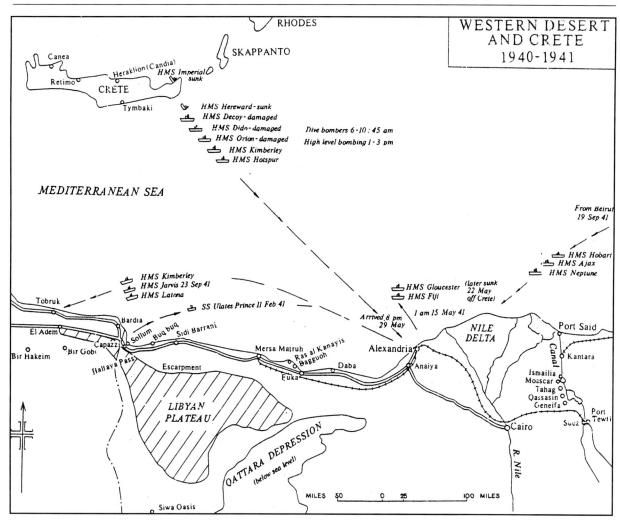

WESTERN DESERT
AND CRETE
1940-1941

RHODES

SKAPPANTO

Canea

Heraklion (Candia)
HMS Imperial
sunk

Retimo

CRETE

Tymbaki

HMS Hereward - sunk
HMS Decoy - damaged
HMS Dido - damaged
HMS Orion - damaged
HMS Kimberley
HMS Hotspur

Dive bombers 6 - 10 : 45 am

High level bombing 1 - 3 pm

MEDITERRANEAN SEA

From Beirut
19 Sep 41

HMS Hobart
HMS Ajax
HMS Neptune

HMS Kimberley
HMS Jarvis 23 Sep 41
HMS Latona

SS Ulates Prince II Feb 41

HMS Gloucester
HMS Fiji

(later sunk
22 May
off Crete)

Tobruk

Bardia

El Adem

Sollum

Buq buq

Capazzi

Sidi Barrani

Arrived 8 pm
29 May

1 am 15 May 41

Alexandria

NILE
DELTA

Port Said

Bir Hakeim

Bir Gobi

Hallaya Pass

Escarpment

Mersa Matruh

Ras al Kanayis

Bagguoh

Fuka

Daba

Anaiya

Kantara

Ismailia
Moascar
Tahag
Qassasin
Geneifa

Port
Tewfi

LIBYAN
PLATEAU

Cairo

Suez

R. Nile

Canal

QATTARA DEPRESSION
(below sea level)

Siwa Oasis

MILES 50   0   25   100 MILES

was, I could feel the blast of the bombs and hear the people shouting and screaming.

On Tuesday 20th, over came the Paras and all hell let loose. I was the company runner. I was in a slit trench with my Company Adjutant when he sent me down to the company office. When I arrived

Chindits

Port Said, Egypt on leave after Crete - June 1941. Harry Slaney (right) and friend.

two water bottles and made my way back to the trench.

We cleared the immediate area of Germans. I handed the cash over, glad to still be alive. We lived on a knife's edge. On the night of the 29th May, a Sergeant came up and whispered very slowly and clearly: "We are leaving Crete tonight". My heart skipped a few beats and I could hardly restrain myself from shouting out loud with sheer joy and relief. We abandoned our heavy kit, except rifles and haversacks. I got rid of my groundsheet and in its place I put a leather writing wallet which I still have.

We crept down to the docks that night where we were taken out to a destroyer. We had no sooner settled down when we were told we were moving. We were transferred to H.M.S. Dido. I found out later that the destroyer had run aground and had been disabled. This caused some delay, allowing us to be caught in broad daylight still within range of the German divebombers.

When I first arrived on board Dido I was sent down to 'A' mess deck which was under 'A' gun turret. I found myself sitting next to an Australian soldier. I had saved my autograph album and so I got him to write in it. He put the following words:- Pte Dunshea I.A. NX 14139 2/4 Btn AIF just out of Crete 29/5/41. I cut this out and sent it home to my girl. We still have it in her scrapbook. He offered me a drink of rum out

there it was on fire and I used an Officer's great-coat to put it out. I collected all the P.R.I. Money and stuffed it down my shirt front. For a while I felt that I was the richest man on the island. I filled our of a stone jar but I refused. I wanted to know what I was doing if anything was to happen.

Shortly afterwards there was a terrific thump and the ship shuddered. A calm voice came over the tannoy saying: "It's OK lads, it was only a near miss." The Aussie said: "It was that much of a near miss I saw the flash through the plates". No sooner had the words been said when there was another almighty crash. Through the door into 'B' mess, there was a mass of flames. At that moment I came as near to committing suicide as I have ever done. Then I thought what the hell! If the Ities and the Germans couldn't get me why should I help them out? So instead, I said to the chap next to me: "Here, hold my hand quick!" He obliged. We sat there as told to by the sailors, and in a matter of minutes they had the fire out. It was some time before they cleared the dead. We finally limped into Alex. The whole convoy had taken an awful bashing.

There were several sequels to the Crete do, and one of them was pretty quick in coming. Within twenty days we were on our way through Palestine to fight the Vichy French in Syria. Just before we moved over the border, an order was sent round asking for the names of everyone who had been on Crete. Good! we thought, we're going to get a medal. Not likely. We were stopped two shillings and sixpence out of our pay towards NAAFI losses.

We weren't allowed to call the Vichy French the enemy, only the opposition. Although the fighting only lasted three weeks, there were over 100 battle casualties. No sooner was it over than one of our blokes got twenty one days detention for refusing to salute one of their Officers

September came and we were put on twelve hours notice to move. We left for Beirut, onto HMS Hobart to Alex. Three days later we boarded HMS Kimberly, Jarvis and Latona landing in Tobruk late at night. 425 of us relieved over 1000 Aussies. I can recall months later we were amazed by the headlines in the English papers which stated:

'Fresh and eager British Troops relieve the Aussies in Tobruk.'

One day I was standing near to my platoon Officer as he was talking to another Officer who said: "I wish I could get my hands on the idiot who burnt my great-coat on Crete. It cost me quite a few ackers to get it repaired in Cairo." I then knew whose coat it was that I'd used to put out the fire. Of course I didn't say anything.

Before we were relieved three months later, I had the sad task of identifying seven men from 'C' Company who had been engaged on a night attack. One of them was the Sarge. who had led us down to the docks on Crete. Another was a young Officer who had been taken prisoner once and escaped from Greece via Turkey where he had returned to his unit.

Chindits

Harry Slankey with friends. Germany - 1945

We returned to Egypt in Jan. 1942 and by February 4th we were on our way through Palestine to Syria. We had been issued with Battle Dress and all thought we were on our way back to Blighty. It's a good job we had Sarge. because there was a blizzard and our tent blew down. March 6th we had returned to Egypt where we were issued with new tropical kit and by March 16th we arrived in Ceylon on board the 'New Amsterdam'

I still believe that we were only sent there as a precaution. If the Japs ever invaded, it couldn't be said that it wasn't protected by the troops. Apart from a bombing raid not long after we landed, we saw nothing.

February, 1943 found us in India, where we later that year trained to become Chindits. By the following year, February 8th, we started out on a 630 mile trek into central Burma from the Ledo Road. As we reached the Chindwin, a message was received from General Wingate. It read: "Well done Leicesters, Hannibal eclipsed". Here we built airfields using only shovels and machetes so that later troops and heavy equipment could be flown in.

Returning to India on April 30th, I saw Vera Lynn. I returned home in October, 1944 where I got married to the girl whose photo I rescued. By June 1945 I was sent to Germany until my demob in 1946.

I met Vera Lynn again at a Burma Star Reunion at the Albert Hall in 1975. I mentioned that I'd met her before and she said to me: "It's taken you a long time to ask for my autograph hasn't it?"

**Ex Chindit Pte. 4860436 Slaney W.H.
SOUTH WIGSTON. LEICESTER.**

Escape by Sampan

"Extracts about the disastrous 'Malayan Campaign, 1941-1942:

On or around the 12th February General Wavell, G.O.C. of British troops on the island, aware of the fact that the island was doomed, relayed the following signal from Java:

"Before the final cessation of fighting, opportunity should be given to any determined body of men or individuals, to escape by any means possible but they must be fully armed."

To my knowledge there is no evidence that any Commander passed this signal on to the troops. No doubt, with ninety thousand massing in Singapore with no evacuation plan, this would have created panic, yet escape was possible.

Early morning of the 14th February I found myself, along with two other members of my Battalion, almost in the vicinity of our own Gillman barracks, having been cut off from our Company during the night of the 13th February amidst heavy fighting and confusion. Bren carriers were racing down the road with troops clinging to them moving away from the advancing Japanese.

Australian, Indian and our own British troops were roaming about at random, completely confused and demoralised. We were later to meet four more of the Loyals Battalion who had also been cut off. We stopped a dispatch rider for any news; his information was anything but hopeful. He told us he had just returned from Fort Canning, Singapore, where an important meeting was taking place with the Chiefs of Staff. Rumour was that it would only be a matter of hours before we were forced to surrender to the Japanese as the water supply to the island of Singapore was completely cut off.

The situation was indeed grim. We had reached the stage whereby we had two alternatives: imprisonment by the Japanese with the possibility of execution, or we attempt an escape. A million to one chance: the seven of us agreed on the latter.

On the 15th February, at the break of dawn, we made our way to Keppal Harbour. As usual, the harbour was full of stationary sampans, countless boats and small crafts. We scrambled aboard a sampan despite the protests of the owner, a Malayan fisherman. After bribing him with cigarettes, a few Malayan dollars and the promise of a reward on reaching safety, we then put to sea.

We were fully armed with one tommy gun, a couple of drums of ammunition, six rifles and fifty rounds of ammunition for each. We had no map or compass but one of the men was able to produce from his haversack a pair of binoculars, which he had taken from a dead Japanese Officer during the fighting in Malaya. These were to become indispensable during our escape. We possessed hardly any food but we all had a fair amount of water in our water bottles.

Towards midday on the 15th February, we had made little progress due to the stillness of the air

Escape by Sampan

having little effect on the ragged sails of our sampan. We were only a few miles from Singapore. As we looked back we were able to see palls of smoke and fires burning.

During the day our main problem was low flying Japanese aircraft. We had anticipated this and on hearing the first droning sound of aircraft, we hid under the cover of our groundsheets, while instructing the Malayan fisherman to show himself prominently. This was a daily routine until we were well clear of Singapore and in reasonable safety.

As we approached the first small island on our journey we observed, with the aid of our powerful binoculars, small troop movement. At first we suspected them to be Japanese but on closer observation we recognised them as Dutch East India troops, very much in appearance like Japanese troops. Nevertheless we approached the island with extreme caution. We needed supplies desperately. This island was to be our saviour. Our observations had been correct.

We were welcomed by the small detachment of East India troops who gave us ample supplies of food and water, and a rough sketch of all the surrounding islands leading to Sumatra. Their Camp Commandant informed us they had received notification that Singapore had fallen and that they themselves would be able to offer little or no resistance to the Japanese if attacked.

We sailed away keeping close to the coastline and for several days we made good progress, obtaining food and water from the many small islands leading to Sumatra. Several miles before reaching Sumatra we decided to abandon the sampan. It had served its purpose. We would now have to travel overland by any means possible if we were going to reach our destination, India.

We left the Malayan fisherman on the sampan without informing him of our plans. We then took to the jungle. We were now desperate soldiers, knowing it would require all our stealth, cunning and training to survive as we were convinced that by now the Japanese would have fanned out to Sumatra.

Mostly, we travelled by night and rested during the day. At all times during our rest period, there would be two men on guard, one with a tommy gun in case of a surprise attack. Though the odds were stacked against us we were determined to survive, having left behind us seventy days of disorganised warfare.

We maintained discipline and planned every move as a team, solely dependent on one another. Luck was on our side. From constant observations through our binoculars at high vantage points, we were able to watch convoys of Japanese troops on the move. We pushed ahead at all speed, at times with the help of road transport obtained unofficially. Most of the time we travelled on foot using the

Escape by Sampan

dense jungle for safety.

After many adventures too numerous to relate, we eventually reached Padang, a busy little seaport town in Sumatra. We approached it with great caution, observing from a distance very carefully, before deciding it was obviously a safe zone unaffected by the Japanese pinzer movement. There was also plenty of transport available.

We contacted the Dutch officials who informed us that several important personnel were soon to leave Padang by sea and would willingly take us aboard. We were put ashore at Bombay, India and we then made our way to the nearest military H.Q. Koboba camp. For the first time in my years as a regular soldier, I witnessed the Sergeant Guard Commander speechless as he was confronted by seven soldiers, heavily bearded, unkempt and fully armed reporting for duty.

We were issued with a complete change of kit and then interviewed for several days by Officers of the intelligence department. They listened with amazement as we gave them a full account of our escape and the vital information we had collected by observing the Japanese movements in the Dutch East Indies.

We were then congratulated, medically examined and declared fit for further active service.

From Bombay I sent a telegram to my parents to inform them that I was safe in India. A few weeks later, I received a reply by airgraph letter that I had been posted as missing and it was reported in the *Oldham Chronicle* that I was presumed 'killed in action.'

George Moss

On returning to the U.K., after some enquiries, (to the best of my knowledge) I was the only Oldham man to escape, avoiding the hell camps of the Far East.

The men involved in our escape all belonged to my Regiment: 'The Loyal North Lancs'. We were stationed at Gillman Barracks Singapore."

A list of those who escaped......

George Moss.	A Company. Oldham.
Cpl. Worsley.	A Company. Bolton.
L/C. Davies.	A Company. Cheshire.
Pvt. Bibby.	A company. Wigan.
Pvt. Kirkbright.	A Company. Bolton.
Pvt. Clayton.	A Company. Nottingham.
Pvt. Spillane.	A Company. Liverpool.

**GEORGE MOSS.
OLDHAM. LANCS.**

A South Atlantic Incident

"I walked out on to the upper deck of the Fleet Destroyer on the beautiful afternoon of August 3rd, 1942.

Two "N" Class Destroyers, the Australian 'Nepal' and the Dutchman 'Tjerkiddes' were the anti-submarine escort to the troop convoy of several large liners. Troop convoys, with big ships employed, are fast convoys and this one was no exception. In the distance on the port side, the Dutchman's huge bow wave was plainly visible.

The ships were bound for the Middle East around the Cape of Good Hope, where the safe arrival of the Armoured Division they carried would greatly influence the outcome of the Battle of El Alamein. Steaming in the centre of the convoy could be seen the Cruiser 'Orion'. She too, was on her way back to the Med after a major refit. The three bombs that badly damaged her during the Crete evacuation penetrated her decks killing several hundred soldiers sheltering below. A gentle breeze blew across an almost calm sea with the nearest of the two great liners the 'Windsor Castle' and the 'Arundel Castle' presenting a magnificent view.

Conditions were excellent for the off duty watch to sunbathe, so I walked down and climbed the steel ladder that led to the twin 4.7 Gun Turret where the guns crew were closed up in second degree readiness. Seeing several dolphins playing in the ships wake was the last thing I remember before

I dozed off into a restful sleep. Sometime later in the dim distance I heard one of the gunners make a remark about a string of flags flying from the foremast. In a suspended animated state my brain told me: "That's the twelve minute alter course signal for the zig-zag manoeuvre." Then came another remark: "There is a large black flag being hauled aloft now." "What's a large black flag?", I was asking myself. As a radio operator, flags were not my scene, but I did tangle with them during my basic training in Depot.

It came to mind: "Am in contact with an underwater object" - a submarine! Leaping to my feet, I sprinted forward and headed for the Wireless Office just as the alarm bells rang and the starboard lookout yelled: "Torpedoes on the starboard bow!" The tracks crossed our bows heading for the Windsor Castle. But the great ship was already altering course to port, so the torpedoes sped by her to harmlessly comb the convoy. Picking the wrong moment to attack, the Submarine Commander must have cursed his bad luck. Guided by an Asdic bearing and a track to follow, we sped along it at high speed to drop a pattern of depth charges. The port-side was almost awash as the ship turned about and slowed down in a creeping attack. It was a cat and mouse game. Another contact, so the destroyer moved forward towards the submarine until the transmitted Asdic pulse and the echo were almost one. Out went the port and starboard depth charge throwers and three 300lb charges dropped from the stern. Fifteen hundred pounds of high explosives erupted below, tossing columns of water high into the air.

Again we turned and slowed down. Minutes went by with the ship creeping towards the contact. Then gathering speed again, the destroyer moved forward to fire another pattern of charges. This time, huge air bubbles came up to the surface followed by an oil patch that spread over a large area of the sea. There was a sudden quietness as we all gazed at the scene, knowing full well that some ninety men were either dead or in real trouble deep below us. After a while, the Asdics reported the faint submarine echo had faded away. It was then that Commander Morris gave the order to rejoin the troop convoy, which at high speed had already disappeared over the horizon.

The quarter-master could be heard piping through the mess decks: "All hands to tea." But my mind was still on the submariners below. Rostered for the first dog watch, I walked into the Wireless Office to take over the watch fifteen minutes before time.

Even the thought of - it's them or us - can't justify erasing these incidents from one's memory banks. Perhaps it is made a lot easier when the scales are weighed against the hundreds of soldiers that might have drowned if the torpedoes had found the target.

We were told later that this action was classified by the Admiralty as a most probable sinking of a submarine."

**LEONARD J. COX.
HIGHBURY. AUSTRALIA.**

The Assault On Madagascar - 5th May 1942

"Little publicity was given to the landings and occupation of Madagascar but the success of the whole operation was paramount.

In 1941 with Field Marshal Rommel advancing rapidly in North Africa and German and Italian sea and air supremacy in the Mediterranean, supplies and reinforcements to the Eighth Army in the Middle East were shipped from the UK around the Cape of Good Hope and through the Mozambique Channel. Much shipping was lost on this sea route with the Germans suspectedly operating from Vichy controlled Madagascar. Coupled with this, Japan had captured Singapore, sunk the Battle Cruisers 'Prince of Wales' and 'Repulse', were gaining control of Burma and rapidly progressing towards India, the Indian Ocean, Africa and the Middle East.

It was at this stage, that Winston Churchill personally gave instructions that Madagascar must be occupied at all costs to diminish the sinking of merchant ships bound for the Middle East, and to prevent Japan gaining a foothold on Madagascar, thereby controlling the air and seas adjacent to South Africa.

One of the many assault landing craft carried by 'Mother Ships' 'Karanja' 'Karen' and 'Winchester Castle'. Each used to transport 30 commandos to the beachhead.

The Assault On Madagascar - 5th May 1942

Thus, the combined operations 13th Assault Flotilla was formed, consisting of 'Keren' and 'Karana' carrying Landing Craft Assault; 'Sobieski' (A Polish vessel) carrying beach assault craft; 'Derwentdale', with specially constructed gantries carrying Landing Craft Mechanical (15 in number) and 'Winchester Castle' (20,000 Tonnage) being the largest ship, carrying Landing Craft Assault and Senior Officers.

The flotilla joined a large convoy and sailed from the United Kingdom on the night of 23rd March, 1942 bound for Durban, South Africa. Here, the assault force was joined by a Royal Navy protective screen, consisting of the Battleship Ramillies, two Aircraft Carriers, two Battle Cruisers, Destroyers, Corvettes and Minesweepers.

Here (unlike later wartime landings usually timed for daybreak following gun and rocket barrages) it was earlier and generally considered that darkness, quietness and surprise were the best methods of attack. Furthermore, rocket ships infantry and tank landing ships, utilised as the War progressed, were virtually non existent at this stage.

The huge land-locked harbour of Diego Suarez and Port of Antisirane, Madagascar were the primary objectives, all protected by strong seaward defences, mainly French 75 gun emplacements. We later learned the controlling Vichy French Government considered attack from the rear of the harbour unlikely as the coastline was extremely rocky and

Reg Voller (centre) and friends after the landings were complete at Madagascar

virtually un-navigable for many miles.

The landing and occupation was scheduled for the night of 5th May, 1942 at 0200 hrs which fortunately was a very calm sea and pitch black. There was no moon. The five unlit assault ships, leaving their protective Royal Navy screen, headed towards the coast proceeding slowly and on line ahead. Orders were given: "Lower all Assault Crafts complete with Commando Forces and Mechanised Units to within six feet of the waterline".

The outline of the nearest ship ahead was only faintly discernable as we stealthily sailed onwards, each with our own private thoughts. How long

The Assault On Madagascar - 5th May 1942

before we were discovered? Sitting ducks silhouetted on searchlights, then a gun barrage perhaps. What reception awaited us as we beached with our landing craft?

Suddenly, in the distance, a pair of dim lights appeared ahead with more pairs stretching far away in the darkness and our ships still in line ahead, sailing on, taking a long winding course between each pair of lights. The only sound on that night air was the faint throb of ships engines and the swish of water.

Eventually, our ships hove to. Anchors were released as quietly and slowly as possible and orders were given simultaneously in all ships to complete drop and release all landing craft. They in turn, fully loaded with Commandos and equipment, headed for faint guide lights on shore, off-loaded and thereafter, made return trips to and fro with soldiers and equipment.

As daylight gradually came, we discovered we were in a large bay called Courrier Bay surrounded by jagged rocks as far out to seaward as we could see.

I never found out when, how or who placed those lights. Each pair was cleverly shaded from the shore, which marked our channel through those treacherous rocks that dark night. The success of the whole assault was dependent on them alone it was a well-planned, clever manoeuvre, enabling us to land forces and attack the port and harbour in the rear of its defences.

Within four days the Commandos and supporting army had completely secured control of their objectives ashore, and our five Assault Ships moved from Courrier Bay to the land-locked harbour of Diego Suarez, rejoining the Ramillies, Destroyers Corvettes and RFA oil tanker 'British Liberty'. Our first view of the port installations revealed a German ship, holed and lying on its side in dry dock obviously our Commandos' handiwork.

Winston Churchill's assumptions were correct as within a week a Japanese midget submarine penetrated our Corvette harbour entrance screen sinking the 'British Liberty' and severely damaging the Ramillies with torpedoes. Gunfire lasted into the night and the submarine crews, unable to escape through the sealed off harbour entrance, attempted to land and disperse in the adjacent jungle. However they were all rounded up and efficiently dealt with by our Commandos.

Various landings followed at other ports of Madagascar, and this diminished shipping losses in the Mozambique Channel and Indian Ocean. For the record, this was the first combined operations landings of World War Two that culminated in permanent occupation.

The men of the 13th Assault Flotilla eventually were involved in landings in Burma, Sicily, Salerno, Naples, Anzio and Southern France before returning to the UK."

E.G. VOLLER. WEYMOUTH. DORSET.

Two Sisters

"This is the true story of two destroyers, 'Ashanti' and 'Somali'. They were sisterships - were, because the 'Somali' was escorting with 'Ashanti' a convoy from Archangel Russia to the U.K. For seventy two hours, 'Ashanti' and the ships company did their utmost to save their wounded sister. What happened during those hours gave me nightmares for many years afterwards.

It was nearing the end of September, 1942. We had already been part of the Fighting Destroyer Escort on three previous convoys to Russia. Also, we had in August been escorting the famous Pedestal Convoy to Malta.

We were on the homeward bound convoy and as our destroyer 'Ashanti' was leader, we had to alternate our escort positions according to weather conditions. In the early hours of the morning we had changed positions with 'Somali' and were about 120ft ahead of her when she was hit in the engine room and boiler room by two torpedoes from a U-Boat. The hole in her was as large as a double decker bus.

Smoke and steam were bellowing from her and she listed heavily to starboard. We thought she was about to sink.

'Ashanti' immediately swept around and dropped several patterns of depth charges as a mine sweeper went alongside 'Somali' and took off about 100 merchant seamen survivors, 140 Officers and ratings, leaving about 80 other Officers and ratings still on board.

'Somali' didn't sink. Commander R.G. Onslow, C.O. of 'Ashanti', decided to tow her to Iceland. A very long tow. Eventually, after two unsuccessful attempts, we now had 'Somali' in tow moving at roughly five knots. Meanwhile the remainder of the convoy had gone on, leaving the two sister ships alone.

We were eight miles S.W. of Jan Mayan Island. The temperature was about 25°F with an icy wind blowing and very soon the snow began to fall. As we crept along, we tried to ease 'Somali's' passage by pumping oil over the stern, but after an hour the tow parted again. We managed to rejoin the cables despite the weather conditions. 'Somali' was asked: "How are you feeling?" The reply was: "Quite well, thank you."

All hands were kept at Action Stations and except for staggered watch changing no-one was permitted to sleep. At the speed which we were moving, we were a sitting target. For the next three days and nights, we plodded on. Although the orders were no sleeping, we were cat-napping whenever possible.

At dawn of the second day, Commander Onslow sent myself and nineteen other ratings over to 'Somali' in the motor cutter to help to cut loose her deck equipment, dump her ammunition, oil and as much top gear as possible. She was without lights and heat. Her steering was out of action and

Two Sisters

her port turbine had fell out making her list to starboard worse. She was by now completely water-logged astern.

During the remainder of that day, we ran an emergency power cable to her. It was a hard, cold job, but when we'd finished, the working party returned to 'Ashanti'. When the light went on 'Somali' sent us a message saying: "Many thanks, sister." During the evening we also attached a telephone wire so the two C.Os could talk.

The third day went quietly and everyone was full of hope. All we thought of was saving 'Somali' and getting some sleep.

During the night the weather became very heavy; waves ran very high with white tops and very deep troughs causing the towing cable to part again taking with it, of course, the power and telephone cables. With the weather as it was, this was not altogether unexpected. 'Somali's' Aldis lamp flashed: "Close in. I'm sinking. Goodbye."

Two Sisters

With our searchlight on her we watched the stern go down first. The bow lifted and pointed upwards as we watched men jumping off into the cold sea. She sank very fast. The scrambling nets were put over the side but we dared not stop the engines as part of the tow cable was still streaming astern. We all did our utmost to spot and pick up survivors. Some were throwing life belts and codlines. Half a dozen others and myself were at the bottom of the scrambling nets up to our waists in the icy water.

As the searchlight spotted the men in the water, (it was so clear you could see their legs and arms) we tried to grab them. When we missed, lifebelts and lines were thrown to them. They were either too frozen or dead and did not respond. Between 30 and 40 men floated past out of reach. A life raft came near us and we grabbed it. There were three men on it, one was an Officer. We hooked the Officer. His name was Lt. Bruce. He refused to be brought aboard. He was determined that we took the men first. Sadly, by then, the raft was sucked away under the ship. If ever a man gave up his life for his men, Lt. Bruce did. We rescued thirty five survivors. The searchlights kept scanning the water for three hours but no more were found.

The last man to be pulled from the water was unconscious. He was taken to the bridge to the Captain's sea cabin. It was Lt.Com. Maud. After about twenty minutes in the warm cabin he started to sing at the top of his voice. Afterwards he told us that this was the only way he could stop himself from freezing. He had no knowledge that he had passed out in the icy sea. There is little doubt however that a fair share of Pussers Run helped a lot.

One of the seamen had been to the galley and taken a jug of 'Kia' (cocoa) on to the bridge. While filling a mug to give to the frozen Officer, he spilled most of it onto his legs. All Lt. Com. Maud said was: "More please."

The next morning he was on the bridge with Commander Onslow as right as rain. Although everyone was dead beat, none of us could sleep much because we were haunted by the thought of the men we had watched float by us frozen and dying, those we had been unable to save. We couldn't forget them. It could just have easily been us.

Coming into Scapa Flow, we heard terrific cheering from the ships in harbour. I heard one A.B. say to another: "Who getting the cheers then?" He replied with surprise in his voice: "Blimey, it's us." We all went up on deck and sure enough, every ship in harbour had its rails lined with cheering men waving and throwing their caps in the air. It was all for us. It did make us feel a little less downhearted."

REG SWAN. GRIMSBY. S.HUMBERSIDE.

A Wooden Story

1943 **6th June, 1943**

"We were in the desert at a place known as Knightsbridge. Nothing there but sand. Merely a name on a military map. I was an NCO in a signal section attached to a regiment of artillery (25 Pounders). The day before we had been told to dig in. This was the start of Rommel's big push that lead to Alamein.

On the 5th June, tanks of the 7th Armoured Division had gone in to attack Rommel but they were outnumbered and forced back through our lines. We were ordered to hold the enemy up as long as possible and by the morning of the 6th we were completely surrounded. The enemy tanks fired into us from all angles and by late afternoon, all our vehicles and guns had been hit.

The order was given to destroy everything which may be of use to the enemy. I had burnt the code books and I was busily destroying the wireless set with a pickaxe head when I heard a voice behind me. I didn't understand what he was saying, but when I looked around and saw the German with his machine-gun pointed at my back, I knew exactly what he meant. The set was already destroyed so I stood up and joined the growing column of P.O.W.s.

We set off on our long march with tanks on either side as escort. For three days, we had neither

CHAPTER 6

A Wooden Story

food nor drink as the enemy had only enough for their own men. On the second day we were machine gunned by our own fighter planes. A squadron with sharks painted on their fuselage. They probably thought that we were German Infantry pulling out for a rest as we were escorted by tanks. Some men tried to take cover at the side of the tanks. Some were wounded as it was the tanks that the planes were attacking. I made a dash to the side, out of the line of fire and then realised afterwards that I might have been shot by the tank gunners had they thought that I was making a break for it. The pilots soon saw that we were P.O.W.s, and after waggling their wings, flew off.

On the third day some men who had collected discarded tins drank their own urine. Our tongues were dry and swollen. Later we came upon an Italian camp. Outside one of the tents there was a water barrel. One of our men held out a small tomato tin and indicated to a soldier standing near the barrel, that he would like some water. The Italian filled the can but before releasing it, he indicated that he wanted the ring he saw on the man's finger. A German soldier who had been with us throughout our hardship saw this and taking the can off the Italian, gave it to the POW at the same time slapping his open hand across the Italian's face. As you see, there were good and bad on both sides.

I recall a story that some Australians had captured a number of Italians. After previously hearing of their own men being ill treated by their captors, the Italians were made to sit within the confines of a circle of stones as there was no internment camp close by. They were warned that if any of them stepped out of the circle they would be shot immediately. During the night the Australians shot the lot of them and moved the stones.

Eventually, we arrived at a holding camp, where we received food and drink. Some of the men were desperate for a cigarette. Here, 'the mother of invention' came into operation as blotting paper was used for cigarette paper and coffee beans were used for tobacco. As you can imagine, a lot of men were taken ill.

Came the day of embarkation to Italy, we were shipped out on an old coal boat and were cramped up in the hold. There were one of two panics over air raid alarms and eventually, we arrived at Naples. It was evening. The Italians did not want us to disembark until daylight so that they could parade their captives in front of the locals (although we were not captured by them.) We were told to bed down for the night only to be disturbed again as they brought strong lights to continually shine down into the hold. This made it impossible for us to sleep.

We all kept shouting until finally they took away the lights. As we settled down, I felt cold, clammy feet over my face. It was a rat. Everybody was shouting again: "Rats! Rats!" They were everywhere. People were trampling over each other to get away from them in the dark. We shouted to fetch back the lights but we were ignored. The Italians took no notice of our cries and just let us suffer.

The following morning we were marched through the streets of Naples as we were spit upon by the crowds. We shouted to them: "We'll be back for you one day." And we were.

After a short term in a camp at Capus, we eventually arrived at a camp built to house a few thousand prisoners, Masserata. This camp had a P.O.W.s magazine issued in England to let our relatives know just how well we were being treated. It stated that on the camp there were two swimming pools. A true statement sure enough, but there was never any water in them at any time. Just empty tins.

Our daily ration of food was a cup of lookalike coffee that was very hot and welcome; to those who needed a shave that is; a piece of bread about as large as a hot cross bun; a piece of cheese two fingers wide and a half inch thick and in late afternoon, something they called soup. A large bin like the old type dustbin, was filled with water and a few cabbages were chopped and thrown in. I can never remember any meat or carrots being added. The Red Cross parcels were very welcome. We were allowed one parcel a week when available. Many times they were not.

During a time when they were regular, auctions were set up where you could swap items from your parcel that you didn't like, for something you did. Of course this activity brought out the rats amongst us. One man offered a tin of bacon for a Yorkshire pudding mixture. The swap was made but when the packet was opened, the Yorkshire pudding mix had been replaced with sand.

Sometimes there was tea in the parcels. Some of the more inventive of us made cookers or stoves by cutting tins up to make the fan and sides of a stove, the two lids pressed together to make a pulley. Connecting the pulley to the fan created enough draught to blow the wood into a fierce flame. However, there was only one problem with this. Shortage of wood. As the beds were made of wood, four uprights and three lots of slats to make three beds, it was easy to guess where it was to come from. It was soon discovered that one or two slats could easily be removed still allowing the body to be supported quite comfortably. It was commonplace to see a bed sagging due to the removal of too many slats.

When wood once again became a problem, we had to look elsewhere. But where? We then realised that the sentries used a hut to stand in whilst they were on duty and guess what? Yes! It was made of wood.

That night, as the guard in the inner compound was approaching the end of his beat, six of us

A Wooden Story

nipped out and nicked his hut and hurriedly carried it back to our dorm. I still regret not seeing the sentry's face when he returned to find his hut missing. Or better still, when he reported the same to the Guard Commander. It wasn't long before he, along with a number of guards, came looking for their hut.

By this time though, it had been whittled down as the men attacked it like ants with home-made knives and chisels storing the pieces under beds and in empty red cross boxes. As they were looking for a hut, it was quite easy to fool them. In the camp there were about five thousand prisoners and the next day we were all deducted one lire from our measly biscuit money.

I remember two men attempting a daring escape. The perimeter of the camp was a high stone wall with machine gun posts at intervals. Within this there was a high wire fence which had armed sentries at the corners. Then there was a trip wire about ten inches high over which we were not permitted to step. A P.O.W. did so once while playing football. He was only trying to retrieve the ball when the sentry shot him, even though it was obvious that he was not attempting to escape. It was daylight.

Getting back to the escape, the two men had taken slats of wood that were used to support the mattresses from a number of beds and carved them to the shape of rifles. They were then blackened with dirt of ashes and then they fashioned ammo pouches from cardboard and darkened these also. They were issued with Italian uniforms that had a red band sewn onto the arm. When these were removed they left the arms a bit short but as their arms were bent holding the rifles, it could not be noticed. At dusk, as the guard changed within the compound, they fell in behind them and marched out of the camp.

Unfortunately, they were all caught the following day because they didn't have any passes. The Camp Commandant didn't punish them but he gave his guards the punishment instead.

Eventually, we were all separated and despatched to working camps. I was with fifty others at a camp called Garbagna near Novara, in the north of Italy. I, with another NCO, was appointed joint camp leader and we were called upon every day to receive the orders for the men.

We were sent out every day to work on the farms in groups of ten. We had two Italian guards who always had fixed bayonets. Having a working knowledge of Italian, I passed on the orders from the farmers to the men. We worked for two farmers. One was called Tozi and the other was called Primo Saccho.

We worked alongside old men but the farmers thought that we were working too slow. He made us work with the women thinking that we would be shamed into working faster. He was wrong. The women slowed down instead. When we asked for

A Wooden Story

*The working party
at Garbagna
(Novara),
northern Italy*

food from the farmers we were refused as they said they weren't allowed to feed us.

One day, Tozi asked me why we all worked better for Saccho. I replied it was because he gave us fruit and milk. From that day on he used to give us wine or eggs. Of course he had to give the guards something also. The next day we let slip to Saccho that Tozi was feeding us and of course he then gave us something.

One day, I was asked by one of the men if it could be arranged for him to see a dentist. I saw the Officer in charge who said that he would make the arrangements. Sure enough, a couple of days later, a civilian accompanied by four soldiers came up to me and said: "All those wishing to see the dentist could form a queue." Altogether there were eight men. The first in the queue needed an extraction. As he sat in the chair, two soldiers held his head and neck and the other two held his legs. The dentist (amongst a lot of bubbling and gurgling)

A Wooden Story

then extracted the tooth. He then shouted for the next patient but there was no longer a queue. The lack of any anaesthetic seemed to have cured them immediately.

Came the day the Germans moved into the area, we made a break for it, hiding in cornfields as they fired into them to try and flush us out. We laid low and they finally moved on. We hid at a farm we knew hoping to stay until our own troops arrived on the scene.

After a few days, an Italian Officer arrived who wanted to speak to me. He wanted us to go with him to defend Novarra against the Germans. I refused. At this point he pulled out his gun and pressed it into my stomach telling me that my men and I would be going whether we liked it or not.

I thought to myself that here was a man dressed in full Italian uniform, walking along roads constantly patrolled by German troops and who was unafraid of being picked up by them. He must be a Fascist hoping to gain praise from the Germans by handing us over. He repeatedly tried to make me agree to go with him, and the lads, sensing something was wrong, gathered around us. On noticing them he decided to back down. I realised how close I came to being shot. Not willing to risk the chance of him coming back with reinforcements, I decided to move on.

We all voted that Tozi's farm was about the best place to hide as it was on the far side of the village.

Tozi agreed to let us stop as long as we slept in an old water mill on an area well away from the farmhouse. We promised to work the farm in exchange for food until our troops arrived from the north.

It all went well until one morning, about 0300 hrs, I heard a noise coming from below us in the bottom part of the mill. It was a creaking noise. Someone was working the small handpump and I didn't recognise their voices. I lay for a while (about half a second) and decided to wake Bill.

He was six feet plus with a fist like the back of a pig. He was hard to wake but as he did he shouted out loud. I explained what was going on and he asked as to whether he should wake the rest of the men. I told him that if they made as much noise as he did, that we would all be for it. I picked up the only weapon we had; an old sickle. Bill stood on the other side of the door ready to put the first man through it into orbit. We stood there in the dark whilst the others snored blissfully on and the pump handle went creak-creak. You can imagine how we felt as we were hunted men.

The noise long since gone, we remained there until daybreak.

When the farmer entered the room, he went white when he saw me armed with the sickle and this great big fist on the other side of the door. He explained to us just what had happened during the night. It was only two men from the village who had been out catching frogs and they were washing them under the pump.

One day we were working among the maize when Tozi came up to me and told me that the next farm down the road had some German motorcyclists approach three men and say: "You're English, you're English, you're English". Bang! Bang! Bang! They didn't ask, they just fired. We believed it was because the patrol had noticed that they were wearing shoes. We couldn't walk in our bare feet like the Italians did. We now decided that this incident was a bit too close for comfort. The time had come to move on again.

It was decided that we would travel by road to the Alps but Tozi said that he had heard that men were now trying to escape on the railroad. We opted for his idea. His son told us that he knew a conductor on the train and that he could get us some tickets. Garbagna was a small station which meant we would have to change at the mainline station of Novarra. Tozi's son agreed to come with us that far.

The train at Novarra was a corridor train and all the seats were occupied. The lads stood in the corridor whilst I waited on the platform as Tozi's son informed the conductor that we were on board. When I met him, he told me that the Germans were doing spot checks but he would do his best to warn us if anything was to happen. It was up to us then to make good our escape. He advised me to stay on the platform until the train was ready to leave.

As I was waiting, two German Officers covered in braid and badges approached me. I felt as if I had a big sign above me saying P.O.W. I was dreading them asking me any questions and I felt such relief when I finally joined the others on the train.

I had not been on the train long when an Italian walked up to me and said: "You're English aren't you." I replied in my best Italian (which was rotten): "No, stupido, no!" "Si, si", he insisted. This carried on until Bill of the big fist got on the other side of him. With the Italian nicely placed opposite an open window, I admitted it. He told me not to worry. He had lots of friends in England before the War. He used to fly a plane from Rome to Croydon. He asked where we were bound for. "Domodossola", I said, "on the frontier"

He warned us that the Germans were searching all passengers at Domodossola and that it would be safer to get off at the station before. Villa Dossolar was where he was getting off and we would be safer if we followed him. I told the lads and suggested that they keep in twos or threes so as not to attract too much attention.

Once out of the station, we could see the Alps in the distance. The Italian led us away from the town eventually coming to a few houses. He said that he lived there. I told the lads to keep on going until they came to a track or something that seemed a good starting point for our attempt to cross over.

A Wooden Story

J. Lancaster - 5th India Division Signals

They were to wait until I arrived with any helpful information regarding our crossing.

I went into the house with him. He said that he would try and get a guide to take us over the mountains. He then told me to join the others and wait half an hour by the side of the road and the guide would join us there.

We waited for two hours and we were becoming a little anxious. Was this a trap? Perhaps he was a Fascist trying to claim money for handing us over. Taking no chances, we headed off in the direction of the Alps. After all. They were easy to spot. We climbed higher and higher until we found a hut where we settled in for the night. There was plenty of water and mushrooms around.

We set off again next morning and midday saw us looking down into a valley overlooking a village. Some of the men wanted to go down and buy some vino with the liras that old Tozi had given us, but I insisted that by the time they climbed down to the village, bought the vino and then climbed back up again, they would be totally knackered. Most of them agreed and we carried on.

Ahead of us we saw some houses and as we approached, some small children came towards us. Then they dashed back to the houses to inform the elders that we were escaped P.O.W.s. Soon afterwards, the headman came to us bringing a large cheese, as big as a dustbin lid and about two inches thick. We soon demolished it. When we told him that we were bound for Switzerland, he suggested that we stay the night in the village as it was getting late. We decided to stay and continue in the morning.

He showed us to a small church which had a room at the back just large enough for us all. It was half full of hay, no doubt their winter fodder. We were soon asleep only to be woken again early in the morning by a banging on the door. I opened it and saw the headman stood there holding a hurricane lantern. He seemed alarmed as he explained the reason for his early visit. Some men from his village had been drinking down in the little village that we had passed earlier that day. They had overheard some of the locals saying that they were going to come up here and capture the escaped P.O.W.s to hand over to the Fascists.

We left the church in the pitch black of the night, holding hands in the more dangerous places.

Even so, by the time daylight finally arrived, we had lost one man.

We reached the top of the mountain to find a stone, rather like a gravestone, with the words 'Italia' on one side and 'Swizzera' (or something like that) written on the other side. Just then, a shot was fired. We scattered, thinking how flaming cheeky, firing at us while we were on the Swiss side of the mountains.

A man by the name of McNaughton, and I were stopped by a gruff voice shouting from our side. When we looked, it belonged to a soldier in a grey uniform pointing a rifle at us. We were joined by another. I couldn't understand what he was saying so I showed him a letter I had from England. On it was written Kreigsgefangenpost. The Swiss soldier shouted: "Englander." We were safe."

**J. LANCASTER.
STAXTON. N. YORKS.**

R.A.M.C.

"I was in the R.A.M.C. A special unit of medical personnel. A Major who was a surgeon, a Lt. who was an anaesthetist, three drivers, one batman, and two theatre orderlies.

We were a self contained unit a kind of 'flying hospital,' who were sent 'willy nilly' to where the fighting was, as soon as possible and on odd occasions we would only be 2-3 miles from the Front.

The Landing at Salerno

We landed on September 11th, 1943, D. Day plus two, under a lot of artillery fire and bombing.

Eventually we ended up in an olive grove, where we erected our big marquée, with all our theatre equipment, operating tables, etc. Casualties were coming in from all units, British and American. We tackled the most serious cases. Abdominal, chest, and head cases had first priority.

During operations the 46th Div. General came into the tent and informed Major Parker, that he was afraid that he might have to evacuate everybody, leaving us there to tend the wounded.

Just at that time the shelling was very active from both the Navy and the German artillery. Sad to say the wounded outside lying on stretchers began to panic and badly wounded men were trying to crawl into a slit trench that our drivers had dug.

The Major told me to go outside to try and calm them down. A RSM and I did our best, but it was pretty hopeless and one American Corporal wanted my army knife to kill himself. He had lost an arm.

After a couple of days or so, most of the major operations had been attended to, the rest had been evacuated by sea back to hospital which was in a school in Salerno itself.

On occasions we had rest periods of two or three days to replenish stocks etc. We were resting at a farm when we heard an explosion. Everybody said it was a land mine, but the Corporal and I investigated. Much to our horror we found two Italian brothers, aged 9 and 11.

The younger boy had found a grenade, and had held it to his side and pulled the pin out causing appalling injuries. We got them on stretchers and took them into the farm chapel.

They sent for the family priest to give him the last rites. His injuries were appalling, he had lost both hands, had serious chest injuries, lost both of his eyes and had brain damage. He died about an hour later.

His brother only had leg wounds so we operated immediately on him. We removed three pieces of shrapnel from them."

That was one of the sad facts of war.

R.A.M.C.

A letter from my Commanding Officer to my mother.

Dear Mrs Strangeways,

As you may know, I commanded the 24 FSU in North Africa and Italy, up to the time when I got jaundice last February, and I thought perhaps that you would like to know that when last I saw your boy (my Private Strangeway) he was fine and fit.

I do not know whether he told you or not, but his job in the unit was looking after all the major operation cases that I had done, and he and I got to know each other very well and I gained the greatest confidence in him. It is very exceptional to find a man who knows, almost instinctively how to take care of very sick men, and make them as comfortable as possible after a major operation. It is no easy job, particularly if there is shelling still going on around the camp site, as there was at Salerno and elsewhere. Your boy did a grand job of work there, and I think I was very lucky to have him with me.

Please wish him the very best of luck from me next time that you write.

Kindest regards
Yours very sincerely
Geoffrey E. Parker

**L. STRANGEWAYS. Major, RAMC.
LEEDS. YORKSHIRE.**

Christmas - 1943

"On Christmas Eve 1943, I, along with three other British Signals lads, and our British driver, were attached to a South African Divisional HQ, using our wireless truck for sending messages back to our own unit. We had been with these chaps for five weeks, and had been accepted into that special clan society that prevailed in the Western Desert against Rommel, where everyone, from Officers downwards, were short of basic essentials like water and decent food, and we all mucked in and made light of it.

We were somewhere south of Benghazi, with nothing to look at but sand. The coastal strip is fertile and beautiful all the way along from Dernal with roads, houses, grass, palm trees and other cultivation, and of the course the Mediterranean. Warm for swimming, clean with sandy beaches, but out of bounds for us.

The South Africans had been at Alamein as part of the big push. When we joined them in November, they had suffered some losses in a big battle and had been refitted. So they were a friendly crowd, very interested in where we came from in England, as many of then had English relatives.

Camping with them was very much like our own. Each truck was about one hundred yards from any other to avoid bombings, or strafing by fighter planes. The truck was camouflaged, the webbing giving a small amount of shade from the intense heat of the day. The temperature rose to over 100°.

Christmas - 1943

We wore socks boots, puttees, and a pair of shorts. The cook-house was usually in the inner ring. We were lucky if it was only four hundred yards away, it was often a lot further.

Their drivers were native men, all from the Basuto Tribe. They fed at a different cook-house to us and when not driving, they were on guard duty, running from truck to truck delivering messages or doing any maintenance work required on their vehicles.

After morning parade we would strip off to our shorts, but they would always leave theirs on and just remove their boots. This we found very strange.

They were all very good looking blokes with short cropped hair, and they were always smiling. The white South Africans had no time for them. One white Sergeant was constantly warning us about them. How they would steal the watch off your arm, or the socks off your feet. His favourite was that their fathers and grandfathers were probably cannibals.

We were told that they were not to be trusted. On the contrary, we found them to be very trustworthy and certainly very charming. They would come over to us and talk, whereas they wouldn't be bothered with the others.

Many times they would talk of their homesickness as most of them were all related. None of them could read or write, and as they were all from the same tribe, they never heard from home. They were all conscripted for the duration.

We had been in this location for four days and had got settled. It was a flat expanse of hard sand with 100 foot hills on three sides, not a road for miles, no other amenities, just a grid reference. We had arrived along a track, the vehicles spreading out as was the custom, leaving an area in the middle about the size of a football pitch, which we all used to use for letting off steam, 20-25 a side, kick which way you like, join or leave as you please, last one left picks up the ball.

The sun would disappear in 10 minutes. The moon when it was full appeared so near the ground you felt you could touch it by jumping up. The temperature dropped 50 degrees in half an hour and we were glad of great-coats.

We had been invited that night, by the South African C.O., a Colonel, to an exhibition. He didn't say of what. Twenty turned up at one end of the 'pitch', along with everyone else, sitting on the sand. Lights were forbidden, yet there were four wood fires thickening, to make a square 50 yards wide by 30 yards long around the imaginary half way line.

Into the semi-incandescent light, accompanied by native drums, came the Basuto Tribesmen, in loin cloths, animal skins, spears, shields, head dresses and warpaint. We couldn't see the drummers, but the throbbing sound invaded our minds, insistent and persistent.

Christmas - 1943

There must of been a hundred of these men; they moved in lines, shuffling then stamping, chanting and shouting. The light from the fires was enough to cause large shadows as the tribesmen moved from lines to a circle. Their shields were oval, about five feet long and multi-coloured with tassels (human hair? We shuddered). The warpaint covered their faces, bodies, arms, legs. Their savagery was real.

They moved from one dance to another without stopping; only the drumming varied, from light to very loud, and quick to slow. In some they chanted, in others they waved their spears aggressively, their feet moving in rhythm with everyone else. When they stamped, we felt the tremor.

They staged a mock battle, both sides withdrawing 40 yards apart; the two leaders emerged, shouting to their respective "armies". The drums stopped. There was silence. Then, an almighty shout as the two groups rushed headlong at each other with a clash of shields. The drums began their throbbing. There were screams, cries and shouts. The scene got a bit hazy as the dust and sand began to churn up.

It seemed the "right hand" army had won as the "left hand" army ran away into the darkness leaving bodies which the victors were dragging across to their side. This was real. The victors did another dance round the pile of bodies. There must have been twenty at least. All on top of one another.

It looked ghastly. You could tell it was a victory dance by the exaltation in the carrying of both spear and shield, and spears were being pointed at the bodies as they moved and chanted in a circle.

Perhaps the next formation was in front of the bodies; we never saw them go, but it looked as though the Basutos had got a full house for the finale, where, to the accompaniment of these mind-splitting drums, they chanted and moved towards us slowly but relentlessly, full of menace. Two lines of these barriers, shields forward, spears raised and glinting shoulder high.

They came within 50 yards of us, the fires making the shadows even more grotesque. Drums beating and feet stamping in unison, they threw their spears over our heads to the empty ground behind us. The whistle as they all came simultaneously was not a pretty sound, more like the hissing of a snake shattering our nerves even more.

The fires were dampened as if by magic; the

drums stopped at the same time; we were in darkness, lit only by a semi-moonlit desert night, and tomorrow would be Christmas."

**MR. R.A.BURTON.
WHALLEY RANGE.
MANCHESTER.**

H.M.S. Laforey - The Final Hours

1944 "We are returning to Naples for a boiler clean and a well earned break." The date was March 28th, 1944; the scene, Anzio beach-head; the ship, H.M.S. Laforey, flotilla leader extraordinaire. The speaker, Lt. Boyer RNR, 'Laforey's' gunnery Officer. "Thank God," I murmured. At last there was the prospect of a break from demands which had kept us in action at sea for so long.

We certainly needed it. The preceding three months had been exceedingly demanding, a period in which the Royal Navy had experienced heavy losses. Penelope, Royalist, Janus - to mention but a few 'chummy ships' - all lay on the bottom, after constant attacks from the air.

My heart sang as we headed south to Naples. And in Naples harbour on the morning of March 30th, Lt. Boyer and I were talking idly about our hopes for the days of peace to come, when Jock Abernathy, a big raw-boned Scot, appeared to tell us that Captain 'Beaky' Armstrong - our new skipper - wanted us in his cabin.

What would be his news? A recall to the U.K.? Or perhaps a few days in Sorrento or Capri, just as Captain 'Tubby' Hutton had ordered the previous November, when Naples had suffered a terrible typhus epidemic. No such luck. Our skipper's orders were that we were to proceed with full speed to an area west of Stromboli, where a U-boat had been reported.

CHAPTER 7

H.M.S. Laforey - The Final Hours

After all our tremendous range of actions in the Mediterranean, U-boat hunting was recognised by most as a 'piece of cake'. Had we not sunk the Italian submarine 'Asihangi' off Sicily? And anyway, to operate in an area free from the Luftwaffe's attentions would be a relief in itself.

At noon, just before we arrived in the area where the U-boat had been sighted, we were joined by Tumult, Blencathra, Quantock and Lammerton. And soon the metallic clang of the Asdic indicated we had located our quarry.

Attack after attack failed to bring the U-boat to the surface but as darkness fell, our Asdic team was confident that during the night, lack of air would bring her to the surface and my gun-teams would have the chance of delivering the coup-de-grace.

Shortly before 0100hrs the next day, the message was passed to the transmitting station from the bridge, that the U-boat was blowing her tanks and we were to prepare for 'starshell' firing to illuminate her.

Captain Armstrong, for reasons best known to himself, decided not to sound off full Action Stations. The crew were therefore at Defence Stations, only half the armament manned and many men were asleep in the mess-decks. With hindsight, one can say that many of the 179 men who lost their lives would have been saved, had they been closed up at Action Stations. The order came suddenly to open fire and within moments, night became day, as the starshell illuminated the area where the U-boat would break surface.

"Gunner's mate to the bridge." Sub/Lt. Ticehurst, the youngest Officer in the ship - for reasons that I was never to discover - made the call that was to save my life. When I got there, I found the U-boat was clearly visible on the port bow. Our 4.7 armament was soon straddling the target and when the Gunnery Officer arrived on the bridge, I jumped down over the bridge screen to the 'Oerlikon', determined to ensure that the U-boat's deck was raked with fire in case resistance was offered.

Then came the order to switch on the searchlight. It proved to be the opportunity the U-boat skipper needed. Suddenly there was a deafening explosion and I found myself hurtling upwards and then landing with a thud on the 'Oerlikon's' safety rails.

The U-boat had torpedoed us and I was conscious between bouts of blackness and pain, that 'Laforey' was breaking up in her death throes. I tried to stand but had no movement in my legs. Using my elbows, I managed to propel my body to the ship's side. 'Laforey' was sinking and I clung to the rigging as she started her final plunge. Frantically, I tore myself free and with arms working like pistons, propelled myself as far from the inevitable whirlpool of suction as possible.

Suddenly, like a cork, I was whirled round and round and drawn towards the vortex where our

H.M.S. Laforey - The Final Hours

beloved ship had finally disappeared beneath the waves. Fortunately, my half inflated life-belt kept me on the surface.

Gradually, the black silence was broken with the cries of shipmates, dotted around the ocean. With the whistle always carried by a gunner's mate for turret drill, I began to signal in the hope of collecting the survivors in a more compact group. Unconsciousness intervened and when I came round again, it was to hear the groans of a young London AB clinging to driftwood and obviously in a bad way.

H.M.S. Laforey at the bombarding of the Anzio beach-head - Italy 1944

At odd intervals, shipmates would swim to us to offer words of comfort and encouragement and them swim off to assist others. Two such gallant friends, Dave Barton the PO. Cook and Knocker White, the Yeoman of Signals both uninjured but sadly not to survive, continued to help their more unfortunate shipmates.

After what appeared to be an eternity, I spotted the darker shape of an approaching vessel. Suddenly there were cries of: "Swim you German bastards, swim!" Our would be rescuers, were convinced that we were German survivors from the U-boat, which 'Tumult' and 'Blencathra' had eventually sunk. They were unaware of the fact that 'Laforey' had gone too.

Within moments, I was carefully and gently lifted from the sea and into the boat. Oil fuel fouled my mouth and eyes and hid the tears of relief and gratitude for my rescuers.

H.M.S. Laforey - The Final Hours

I was hoisted aboard 'Tumult', encased in a Neil Robertson stretcher, injected with a liberal dose of morphia and despatched to the gunner's mate's holy of holy's, the Transmitting Station. From the usual illegal matelot's hidden resources, a full tumblerful of Nelson's Blood was added to the pain relieving morphia and I sank into peaceful oblivion.

Vaguely, I remember being shipped from 'Tumult' to a waiting ambulance in Naples harbour and arriving at the 65th General Hospital. There, the doctors found I had three spinal fractures. To begin with, I was paralysed from the waist down but my self pity soon disappeared when I looked around the overcrowded wards at our terribly wounded soldiers, being shipped in from their personal hell holes of Anzio or Cassino.

Eventually, after spells in other military hospitals, I was shipped home in the hospital ship 'Somersetshire'. At a hospital on Merseyside there came the never to be forgotten reunion with my dear wife and baby daughters.

After long spells in hospitals and at a rehabilitation centre, I eventually returned to light duty at my depot, HMS Excellent. I finally completed my naval service after serving in Vanguard during the 1947 Royal Tour to South Africa.

After nearly thirty years, I still have deep and abiding memories of 'Laforey' and her crew. Overriding them all is the deep respect and affection for Captain Hutton, who made 'Laforey' and her men into one of the greatest destroyer teams of the war.

The people of Northampton, paid from their pockets around £750,000 for 'Laforey' and events proved their investment was repaid a hundred fold. The generosity of 'Northampton' to the crew, exceeded anything I had previously experienced in the Royal Navy. I shared Captain Hutton's only regret, that the crew never marched through the town when final victory became reality.

I hope that one day, the Admiralty will name another 'Laforey', or 'Northampton' and so maintain the links formed in the days of war.

A further ambition yet to be realised, is to make contact with any of the 17 German survivors from the U223 picked up by either 'Tumult' or 'Blencathra' after they destroyed her. I would like to record the missing chapter of life in U223 as her end approached.

Any feelings of bitterness or animosity towards our enemy of 50 years ago, has disappeared. Anyway, U223 proved a worthy and courageous foe. I only hope her survivors have enjoyed the years of peace, with the same happiness and contentment with which I have been blessed."

BOB BURNS. D.S.M.
THORNTON. LIVERPOOL.

Left or Right: A Soldier's Dilemma

"This is not, as the title might suggest, a matter of politics. Rather it was a matter of almost certainly, life or death.

The scene was set in Italy in 1944. The place, by the River Rapido in front of Monte Cassino, around which there had been a lot of fierce fighting, the date, possibly the 12th May.

Our Battalion of Infantry had been moved up near the river a couple of days previously, to prepare for a crossing in small boats. I was part of the beach party whose job it was to lead them with their boats, about a mile up to the riverbank and see them safely across.

On the night of the 11th, the beach party took the first troops down to the river. At about 2300hrs, the artillery barrage started. It was the biggest barrage of the War so far. The noise was deafening but we still had to see to the troops crossing the river. Naturally the enemy opened fire at once and a lot of the men were hit. Some boats were overturned and many men were drowned.

All this time, our party were still going back and forward to the main force, bringing up men and boats under constant shellfire. I must admit that I was scared, as having been wounded only five weeks previously, I did not want another wound, possibly worse this time.

The forward troops had not advanced very far, so our beach party had to stay on our side of the river for a couple of days until a bridge was put up to take tanks and troops. We were still being shelled.

Some of the engineers who were building the bridge were wounded by shellfire. Nobby Clark and I were close by when this happened. In fact, we had to dive in a ditch by their truck. We put a wounded Sergeant on a stretcher and carried him back to a dressing station. This was about a mile back up the road. We left him there for treatment. Nobby went back to the river on his own and I sat outside the dressing station on the side of the road having a smoke and wrestling with my conscience.

It was a question of turning left or right. If I turn right, I'm back with my men. If I turn left and walk away, I would find peace and quiet. I'd be running away, but then how would I live. Where would I get food and money to survive on, and clothes to wear? I knew that lots of men were living like that but I am afraid that I didn't think I could do it.

Then I thought that I would be letting my comrades down. After all, I was an ex Sergeant, with ten years service in the same regiment. I would hardly set a good example. The Army had been my mother and father for ten years. It had fed me, clothed me, and paid me. I had a lot to be thankful for. I had a lot of good friends in the unit and they would not look too kindly on me if I turned and left.

All this went through my mind as I sat there

Left or Right: A Soldier's Dilemma

C. Monks after the battle of Cassino, during a short rest in the mountains - June 1944.

smoking. I thought, on the other hand if I get up and turn right and go back to the river, I shall be going back to the shelling with a possible chance of being wounded again, but at least my conscience would be clear. I could look my comrades in the eye again.

By this time, I had finished my cigarette. My mind was made up. I stood up, put my equipment back on, picked up my Tommy Gun and turning right, marched off down the road back to the muck and bullets.

I never regretted my decision, and as it turned out, I survived the rest of the War without a scratch. So the right turned out to be right. I wonder now if the dressing station had been on the other side of the road, would the left have been right and the right wrong?"

C. Monks East Surrey Regt.
SURBITON. SURREY.

This story took place between 17th - 20th September 1944. Italy.

"After being in hospital with severe shrapnel wounds received when in action with the 2nd Battalion Beds. and Herts. Regiment, during the fourth and final battle of Cassino in May 1944, I returned to my Battalion on September the 17th. I was just in time for a night assault on the formidable Gothic Line on the Adriatic front. The 8th Army was engaged in fierce battles on a thirty mile front, against nine German divisions. They were defending well-prepared defensive positions, created by the TOTD Organisation.

The offensive started on the 25th August, both sides suffering terrific losses. From the many prisoners taken and interrogated, it was evident that the crack German divisions had been badly mauled. The strain of battle of the past three weeks was beginning to tell. Prisoners looked shell shocked, bewildered and dejected. It was considered that if pressure could be maintained a little longer, the whole German defences would collapse.

With this in mind, reserves were brought up, including the 2nd Battalion Beds. and Herts. Regiment, which formed part of the 10th Brigade, 4th British Division. It was to establish a bridgehead over the Ausa river and take the high ground beyond. 'D' Company, our Battalion, was to spear head the attack.

The Beds. and Herts. assembled north-east of Arlotti, a mile and a half from the Ausa. At 2300 hrs, September 17th, Brigadier Shoosmith, (10th Brigade Commander) ordered them to move off.

Prisoner of the Weh - Rmacht.

The actual crossing of the Ausa ('D' Company's objective), was not expected to be difficult. It was to be made without the revelation of our strength by any display of artillery. As the three platoons advanced in single file into enemy territory, searchlights made their appearance, piercing the night sky at a low angle and lighting up the battlefield.

At the time I was a rifleman (acting runner) in 18 platoon, under the command of Lieutenant Norton.

Advancing cautiously for a few hundred yards through ploughed fields, without any interference from the enemy, the leading patrol hit a dirt road. On the far side running parallel was a high railway embankment, with a four foot deep drainage ditch and its natural advantage for the Company's advance was too obvious to miss. Quickly, we crossed the road and soon, the men of the three platoons with Company HQ and stretcher-bearers bringing up

The Gothic Line

the rear were firmly installed within the ditches protective walls.

From then on the advance continued on hands and knees, and at a much slower pace. We were well into German territory and it could be expected that they would know of our presence. It was only when the section leader of the forward platoon held up his hand in a signal to stop that danger was scented. Automatically, he climbed out of the ditch and on to his feet.

From a large haystack to our right (passed by in the forward platoons' advance) a scuffling could be heard, and the distinctive sounds of weapon bolts being drawn. Suddenly, there was a movement ahead in the darkness. Dark figures appeared and instantly shots rang out. The section leader froze for a second of horrified reaction. Staring in disbelief, transfixed by what he saw, he stepped back one pace and opened fire with his Tommy Gun. The startled German soldier facing him opened up at exactly the same moment with his Schmeisser and they both fell dead.

Now the Germans ran forward and from a weapon pit, deep down inside the haystack, German automatic fire swept over the ditch allowing more Germans to come forward, converging from both sides. The walls of the ditch provided a much firmer base for rifle fire which permitted the marksmanship of the Beds. and Herts. to be more accurate. The attack broke up. A lull in the fighting followed and

the long line of bobbing steel helmets remained intact.

After reorganising their forces, the enemy again tried to reach 'D' Company's position. In the confusion of grenade and small arms fire, one of the attackers somehow managed to reach the ditch, hurling himself on top of the crouching defenders. For a moment or two, the crazed German caused quite a flap, it being too dangerous to fire in the narrow confines of the ditch. A scuffle broke out and it was quickly broken up when the butt of a British 'Lee Enfield' rifle was driven into the face of the German with brutal alacrity. Without any ceremony the unconscious German was quickly hurled into the middle of the road.

By now, it was obvious that the enemy held haystack with its dug in weapon-pit was the main pivot of the German attack. We were ordered to destroy it. Soon, phosphorous grenades and belts of tracer were thumping into it. We then held our fire for what seemed like an eternity. Flaming tracer still crackled from the weapon pit. Suddenly there was a quick upward whoosh of flame and heat. The next moment the haystack became an inferno of blazing straw.

The Germans were forced to back out quickly, as gouts of burning straw fell inwards. Bullets kicked up the earth around them. In a mad dash for the safety of his own lines, a German with his clothes on fire ran on screaming: "Nicht schiessen! Wir sind deutsche soldaten!" (Don't shoot! I am a German soldier!) He was almost there when a Bren gave a chatter and the German fell forward with a cry. The Germans were formidable opponents, but it was overpoweringly clear that they were up against a brick wall. The men of 'D' Company waited but there were no more attacks.

This surprise German attack was to be the dominating factor in 'D' Company's failure to take their objective, for the noise of the engagement now put the river defenders on full alert. However, at the time there was nothing we could do about it; it was decided that we should continue with the advance.

This we did after crawling on hands and knees for a few more yards, our protective ditch finally petering out. Wheeling left, we kept on course for the river and in doing so again, found ourselves crossing ploughed terrain. It having rained heavily previous to the attack, and the crouching men saddled with awkward long handled shovels besides the usual paraphernalia of war we found the heavy loam extremely hard going. We started off running in a low crouch but soon ended up slithering on our stomachs.

At around this time of our advance, it was discovered that some medics and signallers belonging to Company HQ, were missing. In the surprise German attack they had been well to the rear having taken no part in the battle. It was presumed they had been left behind in the ditch. I was ordered to go and round them up.

The haystack was blazing away like a torch on the skyline as I set out on my mission. On reaching the dirt road there was ample and horrible evidence of the previous fighting. The zealous section leader who had climbed out of the ditch to be confronted by a German Schmeisser, was lying flat on his back in a grotesque attitude of death close to his German counterpart. So close were they that the soles of their boots were touching.

Whilst propped up against a smouldering German corpse, the crazed German (who having been thrown out of the ditch and survived) had amazingly regained consciousness. He was celebrating his good fortune with pitiful moans and bewildered shakes of the head. I'd no time to wet nurse him now, finding the men was more important.

After finding my bearings on hands and knees, I crawled along the ditch. Eighty yards on I found them. Puzzled and bewildered, they hadn't a clue as to what was going on. When the first shots had rang out, Sgt. Major Kennedy, after ordering them to stay put, had quickly shot off to join the affray.

In the turmoil of battle, he had completely forgotten all about them. They being well trained soldiers and used to discipline had obeyed and were still awaiting the order of command to move out. The haystack was still crackling fiercely as we moved off.

The Gothic Line

I thought that we would never catch up with the rest of 'D' Company for the cumbersome stretchers slowed us down to a crawling pace. What with this and the possibility of running into a German sortie, I was feeling far from happy. Eventually, after rushing the pace a shade faster, we came across the rest of the men hurriedly assembling near the bottom of a steep ridge, under the watchful eye of the CSM. They were shaping up in preparation for the assault on the River Ausa defences.

On handing over my charges to him without any 'ifs' or 'buts', he quickly hustled me in to the ranks of the section that was to lead the attack. Other sections were to follow up in waves if the attack was successful. With an encouraging nod from the Company Commander, in extended formation, the forward section moved slowly towards the crest. It was pretty rugged at the top. I ended up with my body perched precariously over the lip of the ridge.

In complete silence we awaited the command to attack. We had not long to wait. From the Company Commander, a slight nod to the Sergeant Major. A slight pause. Up went the Sergeant Major's hand and over the top we went. Barely had we gone ten yards, when the enemy reacted vigorously with small arms fire. The charge developed with good force. With rifles and tommy guns we returned the fire as best as we could. Things didn't seem to be going too badly until a Spandau suddenly hissed into violent, frightening life, quickly followed by another. Hundreds of bullets were buzzing around like angry hornets and they weren't choosy whom they stung. A long piercing scream from the rear told us that the follow up section were running into difficulties. The line wavered then fell back with heavy fire coming from the front and both flanks. The forward section had no option but to try and join them.

With this end in mind they broke off the attack smartly doing a left wheel that would eventually take them back over the crest of the ridge to safety. I tried to join them but in my glorious gallop, I had gone too far. I was the most advanced of the line with the added disadvantage of being pin-pointed by the German machine gunners. I thought surely this must be the end as a stream of sparkling re-tracer, came flashing towards me. I felt a violent blow to my head. My knees buckled, then gave out on me.

I tried to raise myself, but the blow to my head had a more pernicious effect than I had imagined. When I was half way up, I paused, wavered, then crashed to the ground unconscious. I don't know how long the Germans waited before deciding to come out of their positions and pick me up but I remember how quiet it seemed at the time.

A medic was in attendance as I was helped to my feet, but even though wounded and incapable of resistance, Jerry was taking no chances. I felt the muzzle of a loaded Luger boring into my ribs, followed by the guttural cry of: "Hande hoch" (hands up). I knew then with complete certainty of body, soul and mind that I was a prisoner.

Escape

There is not much to tell about my escape. Anyone could have done it. It was never the epic it was made out to be. How was it done? Simple. I did it through flattery, cunning and ruthlessness.

I suppose there are worse things in life than having a loaded Luger jabbed in one's ribs by a trigger happy warrior belonging to the Third Reich, whilst tottering down a bleak Italian ridge during the early hours of a cold September morning, but at the time, I certainly couldn't think of one. Half supported by the unarmed medic and the Luger, on tottering legs, I eventually reached the bottom.

By now the rays of first light were creeping over the battlefield and I was very impressed by the outlay of the German defences. A long line of deeply dug slit trenches met my eyes. Heavily manned by automatic wielding Germans and interlocked with heavily sand-bagged machine gun nests. The more I saw of them, the more I realised what a daunting prospect 'D' Company had taken on. At the time I remember thinking how ludicrous

it was that only one Company had been thrown in against them.

In the background, the 'Ausa' was plainly visible, and it looked insignificant to say the least. It had a dry shingle bed with only a trickle of water. From what I could see of it, it didn't seem worth all the fuss, much less a scorching from a German bullet.

Skirting past the last of the machine gun nests, with gawking Jerries staring at me as though they'd never seen an Englishman before, we were brought to a halt by a lurking sentry. Behind him, in a large hollow, lay a cream coloured building. Typically Italian, strongly built, with walls of solid stone, sadly now showing shell scorched gaping gaps. A mute testimony to the accuracy of British field artillery.

In better days, this badly dilapidated building would have been a prosperous farm house. Now shorn of all it's beauty, it had been degenerated to the roll of a German Infantry Regiment's Headquarters. With a flick of the sentry's Schmeisser we were told to enter.

I was prodded down a long flight of stone steps leading into a large dimly lit cellar that in more peaceful days would have been a shelter for the farmer's cattle and poultry. Stone floors where pigs had once lain had been taken over by sleeping German soldiers.

Someone placed an upturned ammo-box in front of me and with a lot of arm waving and guttural

The Gothic Line

noises from my Luger toting escort I was commanded to sit. At least that's what I presumed he meant. I did not understand the words although it was evident from his gesturing and his tone of voice what was expected of me. In the half light afforded me, he looked a rough bugger, a sturdy six foot Austrian with legs like Black Forest tree trunks, with a splash of mouth and penetrating eyes of cold marble.

After my ordeal on the ridge I wasn't feeling too chirpy. My mouth was parched and I felt dizzy. I made signs of wanting to drink; I wasn't fussy, anything would do. With ill-grace my guard got me a mug of water. I quaffed it down and felt better. Satisfied with having done his duty and done it well, the six foot Austrian reluctantly holstered his Luger. After grunting a few words of advice in the medic's ear he then strutted his way up the long flight of steps, pulling aside the blanket that served as a door. I thought: "bloody good riddance" as his backside disappeared from view. He hadn't finished with me yet. Through the opening, a head appeared; he had viciousness stamped indelibly upon his ugly face and he glared with a long piercing stare, followed by the cry: "English Schwein", then he was gone.

It was while the medic was swabbing my head wound, which luckily for me turned out to be an insignificant shallow groove, when into the cellar strode the Commanding Officer escorted by three of his senior NCOs. A dark-haired thick set Major of medium height, over the thirty mark with ample fruit salad on his chest to prove he'd been around a bit.

The Major exuded friendliness; from him came a cynical glance at the bleeding wound. From the NCOs a lot of shaking of heads and grunts of disbelief. The Officer brought forth pen and paper. Ah!. Just my bloody luck. An interrogation in the offing and here's me sporting a dirty great hang-over that any Irish Navvy would have given his right arm to own. As it turned out it was never on the cards.

"I've seen worse concussions" said the Major watching the medic bandage my head. The Officer surprised me greatly by speaking in English, with a strange pronunciation, but with considerable fluency. Then he added, with a twisted smile: "Had the wound been any deeper my young man, a dressing would not have been needed." All the while he was talking, never once did the sardonic expression leave his face. He certainly was a bright spark. Whoever it was who said that the Germans have no sense of humour obviously had never had the pleasure of meeting this one.

No sooner had my wound been cleaned and dressed when a small table was brought forth and placed in front of the Officer. I was then thoroughly searched by one of the NCOs. From out of my webbing pouch the first object was brought forth, one lone phosphorous grenade. Its twin I had lobbed in the haystack. A flicker of interest lit up the Major's face, but the sardonic smile remained. No doubt by now he'd heard all about the 'fire fight' and of the dire consequence concerning the men trapped in the haystack.

After the grenade, there followed the usual bric-a-brac to be found in the battledress pockets of any normal British Tommy. Clasp knife, pay book, fags and matches, etc. But the highlight of the search, was saved towards the end with the arrival on the desk of a neatly tied up bundle of letters. Each one not only bearing my name, rank and number, but also the name of my Regiment. I felt a right twerp, but how was I to know that I was going to be taken prisoner?

With this free information staring the Major in the face, the proceedings livened up a bit. A party atmosphere took to the air. The Officer's sardonic smile turned into a positive leer.

The way he hugged that pathetic bundle of letters close to his chest, any one would have thought that he had found the 'Holy Grail'. In no time at all, it had vanished along with my pay book, into his top tunic pocket. Even the poker faced NCOs gave vent to silly titterings. If they were happy, I certainly wasn't.

It wasn't the fact of them finding out the name of my Regiment that bothered me as I doubted very much if the information gleaned would make the slightest difference in the long run as to the outcome of the War. Of course it didn't. My only crib was that I hadn't even read the damned things. All the letters taken were the ones that had been accumulating in the Battalion orderly room awaiting my return from hospital. I raged inside: "What's the world coming to?" I asked myself. "A joke's a joke, but this is bloody ridiculous". My first night in action since leaving hospital and already I'd been shot, taken prisoner, and as if that wasn't bad enough, now the Germans had purloined my mail. I was really sickened.

As it was, my German captors never did interrogate me. On reflection, it is not hard to see the reason why. During my hours of captivity, I was to see the German Major and his NCOs just one more time. That was during the late afternoon of that same day, September 18th. Up until then, I had seen the German medic pop in and out a couple of times, but he had his own wounded troops to attend to. I also had a visit from my over-zealous Austrian captor, but apart from that, I was on my own. I felt quite isolated and down in the dumps as I hadn't the blind notion of what was going on.

It was while I was having a drag from a German weed, kindly thrown to me from a resting soldier, that the Luger-toting Austrian put in his appearance. Full of vulgarity, he was proudly carrying my steel helmet. I lie; I should have said the remains of my steel helmet. It came out later, he had retrieved it

The Gothic Line

from the ridge whilst under heavy shellfire.

When it was handed around for close inspection, even the battle hardened Germans expressed emotion. There were 'oohs' and 'ahs' and even the odd whistle or two. I too felt like whistling when I saw it (oh, the damage they had done to my beautiful tin hat). There were two bullet holes, plumb in line with each other. The entrance hole was small, neat and tidy; its counterpart a much larger, more jagged affair which said a great deal for German marksmanship, if not for British steel. I thanked the Lord for giving me a thick skull, but most of all, the German machine gunner for only grooving it. I will bless him 'till the day I die.

Even the crazy Austrian joined in the excitement, looking at me with understanding. He didn't stay long. On his departure, my shoulder received a light pat of condolence from a large beefy hand. It should have cheered me up but it didn't. I was missing my own kind. Strutting German soldiers in their camouflaged steel pot helmets were poor substitutes for the lads of 'D' Company. I tried to comfort myself in the knowledge that they would not be too far away and at any minute they would be coming to my rescue. I was having myself on, even a dolt like me.

It was pretty obvious that by now 'D' Company would have left the vicinity of the ridge and would have dug themselves in somewhere more defendable. It would need much more than three platoons of infantry to over run these well-prepared defences.

As it happened, 'D' Company was not all that far away. This I found out later. Having found it impossible to reach the river Ausa against such fierce enemy resistance, the Company Commander wisely ordered them to withdraw. This was done and the men dug in some fifty yards to the rear of the ridge.

During the day, the Company came under heavy attack from a superior German force. It was only on the arrival of a squadron of British tanks, that the men were able to withdraw to a more stable position. In this action, Major Wilson and CSM Kennedy were both seriously wounded. Shortly afterwards, British artillery opened fire on the river positions with high explosives. It was a foretaste of things to come.

Already, 'A' and 'B' Company of the Beds. and Herts., had crossed the Ausa half a mile to the north-west. They were forging ahead in a bid to cut off the remaining enemy held river positions while to our front, the advancing East Surreys were less than a mile distant. Following up the infantry and their supporting armour, poised ready to exploit their success, were '12' and '28' Brigade, each supported by a brigade of tanks.

There was no doubt at all that if '4' Div. could keep up the pressure for a little while longer, the whole structure of the river defences would collapse. It happened that all this was known to the German

Major and most probably the senior NCOs also. No doubt a plan had been hatched beforehand on how to save their own skins should such an emergency arise. One had. It came with dramatic suddenness. It even caught me by surprise.

During the late afternoon, another British stonk rained in on the German river positions, far more accurate than the previous one this time. Screeching British high explosives bracketed the building. In five minutes the cellar emptied, except for a lone sentry nervously pacing back and forth outside the opening. I was alone. It was now that thoughts of escaping crossed my mind. Was it possible? I wondered.

I couldn't help but notice that the pacing sentry wasn't up to the usual standard of German efficiency. Every now and then a large tin potted head thrust itself through the opening, followed by a stare from two sheepish eyes. Then he'd disappear for a crafty smoke. He looked a real beanhead. A great blubbery berk with a flabby chin and a waddle. "Ah", I thought, "It's good to see that the 'super race' has a slug in their camp. That evens things up a bit. Shouldn't be hard getting past him". A bit of cheek, a bit of luck and a miracle thrown in and the dope would be left in his tracks. Then 'hey presto' young Mr. Scully would be back to the safety of the British lines. Anything but this unbearable waiting.

As it turned out, my hastily planned dash for freedom was never put to the test and a good job

too. On looking back, I don't think that I would have stood an earthly. I would more likely have ended up being recaptured and shot. German soldiers didn't believe in taking prisoners twice. In their eyes it was valuable time wasted, but such is the brashness of youth that, at the time, I was all for it. I even still get the 'wobbles' just thinking about it. It's amazing how in the space of a few minutes the course of events affecting one's life, can alter so dramatically, but that's how it happened to me on that late September afternoon whilst the British guns were stonking the Ausa. In fact, it was just ten minutes.

Meanwhile, I was reflecting on the 'pros' and 'cons' of a sudden departure, as outside, the earth was being torn apart by the thundering vibrations. After mangling up the weapon pits, British guns again ranged in on the German headquarters. The first shell to hit the building came with a sudden rush. Exploding somewhere on the roof, more shells followed. Fragments of tiles and masonry showered upon the pacing sentry like confetti. It took him just half a minute to clear the flight of cellar steps. Fear shone from his eyes as he dived on to the blanket beside me on the cellar floor, crouching in a ball as he landed.

A few figures appeared at the top of the flight of steps. Then more joined them. I saw amongst the new arrivals, the German Officer. Surrounding him, looking perplexed and obviously agitated, were the

The Gothic Line

senior NCOs. A heated discussion took place. While this was going on, more men kept crowding into the cellar. I could see by the worried looks on their faces that a British attack against their positions was expected.

The atmosphere was electric. I watched the anxiety in the cellar heat to a cherry glow. At the top of the steps the heated discussion was increasing in 'neins' and 'jas'. A smattering of teuton oaths were being bandied around in abundance by furious NCOs. Through it all, the Officer remained calm and unruffled and the haughtiness of his bearing was out of this world. It was like watching a film and a comedy at that. I use the term comedy in the loosest term possible. I tell you in all my born days, never ever have I seen such a pantomime. It was more toe curling than watching 'Babes in the Wood'.

Displaying arrogant scorn, the Officer managed to take control of the situation. A 'pep talk' followed. No sooner had things quietened down when the Officer looked up as a crescendoing, reverberating howl grew overhead. Almost immediately there was a massed scramble of the holed-up Germans. It was mesmerising to watch. In no time at all, the stalwarts of the 'Master Race' had glued themselves to the floor. Shells burst with violent thuds all around the building and the whole structure shook to its very foundations. I thought it was going to come down on top of us.

A cordite-laden atmosphere filled the interior of the cellar with acrid fumes and men began to cough. The din outside was infernal, the heat inside stifling. I had a quivering churning of the nerves down in my gut. I didn't want to be killed yet. Least of all by my own shells. "It would be just my bloody luck", I said to myself as I wormed my body deeper still into the cellar floor.

At long last, after what seemed an eternity, the shelling fell silent. Cowering men crept out of their corners gazing sheep-faced at one another, amazed that they were still alive. Much more amazing was the fact that during the shelling, the Major and all the senior NCOs had seen fit to make good their escape. It was eerie. One minute they were with us and the next they were gone. They didn't even say auf wiedersehen, see you later, or any of the conventional parting words normally shared between comrades in arms. They just went away. There was no explanation. No apologies or anything.

Not long after, I had a word in the medic's ear about this strange phenomenon. He seemed highly agitated by the whole business. In a strange mixture of fluent Italian, broken English and German swear words, he admitted it was a poor showing on the Officer's part, but declared (rather hastily I thought) that the Major's decamping from the field of battle would have been on direct orders of German high command.

He pointed out (with justification) that in German front line units, Officer casualty figures were much higher in proportion to those of other ranks. In turn, I assured him the same applied in British front line units. I also pointed out (almost rubbing it in) that in no way, higher casualty figures or not, would a British Officer desert his men in time of battle. He smiled, revealing tall, straight teeth, then surprised me greatly by quoting in passable English that schoolboys favourite idiom 'He who fights and runs away'. It seemed to call for something from me, so I said: "hear, hear" and chuckled in agreement.

Already, I had a notion that the future facing me wasn't going to be all wine and roses. For the time being, it would be best for me to float with the tide, and who better to float with than this easy going young medic? He could get me out of the pickle I now found myself in. I would need a friend, German or otherwise. Besides, with him being a medic and all that, he was king of his own cabbage patch. He would hold some sway over the 'common herd'. Yes! I assured myself, he would most certainly be a useful ally to have around. From that time on, I clung to him desperately.

I now took stock of the situation. From what I could gather, what once had been a seasoned fighting unit of well over two hundred Germans, had, in ten days of hard fighting, been whittled down to just over two score men. Including the wounded. Food supplies were non-existent. Medical supplies were running out and now with no leader or senior NCOs to bolster them up, most of the men refused to man their posts. They remained in the cellar shuffling around like ruptured bullocks. Their chances of survival looked very slim indeed.

With all the signs in my favour, I had a notion that there would never be a better time than now to test the possibility of them surrendering to me.

Darkness was creeping into the cellar as I approached the only NCO left amongst them. A tall, ugly, and skinny man. I ambushed him with the most important part of my armoury, bare-faced cheek. Bluntly, I put my notion to him. It went down like a body wrapped in lead. He gaped at me dumbfounded, then laughed. Though how much mirth was in the laughter was difficult to estimate. The others echoed the laughter until he put up his hands. They feared the British attack and quickly cottoned on that in me they had a safe passport for the future and it must be said for the skinny NCO, though sadly lacking in meat, he made up with deceit and cunning.

"The medic's the man to see," he whispered slyly, throwing me a knowing wink. He pointed a bony finger in the general direction of the medic's corner. The medic's eyebrow rose and a thin smile formed on his lips as I appeared before him. "Ah," he murmured fixing me with anxious eyes, "just the man I want to see." He went on to explain that the condition of the wounded was worsening by the hour. "I have no morphine to ease their pain and

The Gothic Line

the lack of food does not help," he added bitterly.

I could see he was a man of high principle and integrity. A man who walked the battlefield unarmed would have need of such things I reasoned. I flopped on the blanket beside him. He didn't look the part. Even in the gloom of the cellar, I could see he was very young. Younger than me, perhaps! His face was unlined. Smooth and fleshy like a baby's, but it was all very deceptive. Under that soft skin lay a layer of steel. It's not often I'm swayed by any emotion but during the next few hours he was to grow on me like a brother. With him there was no need to lay on the charm and jam. We understood each other perfectly.

My main intention was a quick return to the British lines (in one piece if possible.) His was the welfare and safety of the German wounded. We both agreed that the only way these two things could be made possible would be to try and persuade the remaining Germans to throw in the towel. "We'll have to tread very carefully," said the medic, peering anxiously at the sleeping forms around him, "some of the men still think a British withdrawal is possible". "Silly B......S", I thought, while preparing to get my head down, "they've some hopes of that. I know what I think".

There was to be no sleep for me that night. The skinny NCO saw to that. The enemy, though stupid in some ways, were not so stupid when it came to protecting their own skins. Just in case a British attack did come during the night, my sleeping blanket was given pride of place at the foot of the cellar stairs. I tried to sleep but the guards kept waking me. As I nodded off I would hear a sharp "nicht schlafen" (no sleeping). I tossed and turned on the stone cellar floor. I couldn't wait for morning to come. I was up a 0630. There was no sense in freezing to death.

Some excitement was caused when it was discovered that the machine-gun crews had stole away during the hours of darkness, taking their spandaus with them. Also eloped had the six foot Austrian and the skinny NCO, which to my way of thinking, just about left me as 'Commander-in-Chief' and the medic as 'Second-in-Command'. Strangely enough, it so happened this was the way it turned out to be.

The Germans that were left were a motley crew, all except the medic. He joined forces with me in persuading the men that they would be far better off as prisoners of war. We tried very hard. We ran ourselves into the ground as they say, but in all fairness, most of the spadework was done by him. He could be quite persuasive. He was a real charmer, dropping a hint here, flashing a smile there. It seemed to work wonders for in no time at all, his fellow countrymen were eating out of his hand. My part for what it was worth, consisted of telling whopping great lies to the by now infatuated Germans (for I quickly adopted a 'Lord of the

Manor' approach in the cellar). I played the part well.

The fools thought I could walk on water. In no time at all, most of them were in favour of surrendering. There was only one condition, and that was they must all be sent to Canada. It seemed a strange request to me but they were set on the idea. Apparently, they had heard good reports on the 'cushiness' of the P.O.W. Camps in the land of the maple tree. In no way, did I try to dishearten them. If it was Canada they wanted, well, so be it.

Piling on the famous Yorkshire charm thick and heavy, I gave them a solemn promise that I, Private Bill Scully, would personally escort them aboard their ship when due to sail to their chosen destination. The poor mugs believed me. How was I to get them back to the British lines though? That was now my problem. For the next twenty four hours, I was to be their father confessor and Company Commander. Things never quite seemed the same when I reverted back to my old rank of private.

All along the front heavy shelling was continuing from both sides. There was not much hope of us moving out of the cellar that day and no possibility of moving out during the night. We were being torn apart by friend and foe alike. This I told the medic when discussing the problem with him. So it was agreed that unless the British advance reached us beforehand, we would evacuate the cellar at first light the following morning, it being the quietest part of the day.

Around 1700 hrs that same afternoon, sounds of heavy battle could be heard about half a mile distant to our front. The medic and I climbed the stairs to the third floor of the building. From its imposing height we had a panoramic view of the terrain. Through the powerful pair of binoculars we watched the outcome of the battle. It didn't last long. Two Churchill tanks were already brewing up as I swept the terrain. Another sluiced on it's side when hit by a German eighty eight.

I saw the British Infantry, somewhat tiny at that distance, run for cover. Then the stretcher-bearers scouring the battlefield for the wounded. Then the British went to ground. Apparently, they had a battle on their hands. Dimensions were difficult to determine. There was no point in watching any more.

It was time to visit the German wounded. They were on the ground floor, six of them, sprawling around on stretchers. Legs bandaged, arms bandaged, they all had limb wounds except one. "This was the outcome of your attack" murmured the medic with a slight whiff of acid in his voice. I didn't know what to say, so I didn't say anything. The one lying on his back worried me. I figured that someone had done one hell of a good job on his face. I prayed that it hadn't been me.

A bullet had bored through both cheeks

The Gothic Line

removing the tongue on it's way out. All that remained visible were a pair of pain shot eyes and a bloody stump of flesh where his tongue used to be. He was completely bandaged from the neck up. The medic had done a good job. The bandages were that tightly drawn it seemed as though his head was encased in plaster of paris. He must have been a NCO for I could not help but notice the black leather belt complete with holstered Luger that lay at the foot of his stretcher. The opportunity was too good to miss. Whilst the medic was making his way to the cellar, I quickly flipped the heavy Luger from out of it's leather holster into the inside of my battledress blouse. It disappeared.

Strangely enough, no one in the room batted an eyelid or voiced a word of protest although they'd all seen me do it. I thought it strange at the time, but looking back it was highly probable they mistook me for one of the advance guards from the main British force. However, at the time I felt elated. It felt good to have my hands on a weapon again, be it German or otherwise.

It was highly improbable that the Luger would be needed, but I was born with a suspicious nature and a dislike of Germans; however worthy their motives, they were not to be trusted. I discovered later that the Luger was fully loaded. It was still in my possession when, eventually, I reached the British lines. Thus I spent the second night of my captivity in a much better frame of mind than I had my first.

No one slept that night. The excitement was too great. The Germans moved about restlessly. No one spoke.

September 20th. No shelling and a lovely day. Today each man laid down his weapon. They even said good morning to each other, some even whistled and sang. This was the first exhibition of pleasure that had taken place in this cursed spot. I quickly totted up my prisoners. Twenty six including the wounded.

My crowning glory came about an hour later. I had a delightful feeling as I led the long line of Germans out of the cellar. It was the happiest day of my life. There was laughter and acceptance as they began to take up their assigned places, the walking wounded in front with the medic in charge. I reviewed them for the last time before proudly taking my stance at the head of the column. Soldiers of the Third Reich they might be, but they were my prisoners and I loved them all.

Setting out for the British lines I thought merciful God, it's a funny old War I'm having. One minute I'm in the shit, the next I'm floating on air.

For my actions, I was mentioned in despatches. Three days later, the Germans had withdrawn all along the front."

BILL SCULLY. MANNINGHAM. N. YORKS.

The Gothic Line

FRANCONIA
transported
thousands upon
thousands of British
troops during the
War to the Middle
East and The
Mediterranean

Diary, June 19th - August 12th, 1944. Normandy

"X Company Scots Guards attached 3rd Battalion Irish Guards

June 19th.
The 3rd Battalion Irish Guards commanded by Lieutenant Colonel Vandeleur, with X Company Scots Guards attached, boarded ship at Southampton and sailed to a point off the Isle of Wight. The Commander of X Company was Major F. Stewart-Fotheringham. Second in command was Captain E. Hope Llewellyn. I was serving in the No.1 section of No.14. Platoon commanded by Lieutenant ADG Llewelyn.

Ship anchored off Isle of Wight

20th - 23rd.
Sailed towards France and arrived on the French coast at Arromanches, north of Bayeux. We disembarked and marched south to Bayeux.

Resting and sleeping on the outskirts of the town.

24th - 28th
We moved forward, taking up a position in the line between Tilly and Caen. Very quiet. Intermittent shelling of our positions by the enemy. The enemy moved forward at 2200 hrs but they were halted about 300 yds from our positions by terrific artillery fire. They were driven back one mile before dawn.

29th
Quiet all day.

30th
Quiet throughout the day. British artillery began a terrific bombardment of German positions at dusk. The enemy replied by shelling our positions heavily. There were no casualties. A. Company sent out a patrol into the enemy lines.

July 1st
Artillery duels between our own and enemy guns throughout the day. Intermittent shelling of our lines. There were no casualties.

2nd
Very quiet, the enemy now being three miles distant.

3rd
X Company moved forward into a new position roughly about 300 yds from the enemy forward slit trenches. Heavily shelled whilst digging in. Again, no casualties.

4th
Information was given to us that the position in front was Capriceux Aerodrome and that it was held by the enemy. The Canadians, under cover of smoke and high explosive shells, attacked the aerodrome at dawn from a position three quarters

Diary, June 19th - August 12th, 1944. Normandy

of a mile to our left. The aerodrome was captured by noon. The expected counter attack materialised and the Germans regained one half of the aerodrome. A terrific battle raged all day and our positions were mortared and shelled very heavily indeed.

Thanks to the depth of the slit trenches, only one of X Company was killed. There were no wounded. During the remainder of the day, the part of the aerodrome held by the enemy was bombed and machine gunned by RAF fighter planes three times.

5th

A very quiet morning. A slight exchange of artillery fire during the afternoon. Quiet the remainder of the day.

6th

At 0230 hrs. I was on sentry duty in the section Bren-Gun position, when I noticed a number of birds disturbed from a hedge 100 yds in the direction of the enemy. We suspected they were approaching and on being relieved from sentry duty at 0250 hrs, we informed the new sentry of our suspicions. At 0315 hrs. A German patrol penetrated our position, but they were soon scattered, although one member of X Company was shot in the arm.

In the early morning, an enemy tank was spotted on the aerodrome. It was believed to be a Panther.

The distance being about 1700 yds away. A Sherman tank, mounted with a 17 pounder gun was ordered forward to our positions to attack the enemy tank. The platoon was informed that we would probably be heavily mortared when the Sherman tank opened fire on the Panther. The gun crew in the Sherman tank fired six shots but only hit the tank once. It was not knocked out but it rapidly moved out of range. The enemy did not mortar us as expected.

After dark a patrol was sent into enemy lines. During the night the enemy was bombed and machine gunned twice by RAF formations of eight.

7th

Intermittent shell and mortar fire. Otherwise it was very quiet throughout the day. We were heavily mortared and shelled in the early evening. There were no casualties. A mortar bomb exploded, five yards from my slit trench. Luckily, no-one was hurt.

During the day, British bombers, Lancasters and Halifaxs, bombed Caen. I have never seen anything like it in my life. At a rough guess I would say 1000 planes took part in the raid, losing only one. I watched it crash in flames.

8th

Capriceux Aerodrome was still only half taken, the enemy's half being under constant shell and mortar

Diary, June 19th - August 12th, 1944. Normandy

fire all morning. The afternoon was very quiet.

9th

Caen was captured by the Canadians and British at 1000 hrs. The Canadians attacked the remainder of the aerodrome held by the enemy, finally capturing it by 1130 hrs. X Company Scots Guards were still holding the position left of the aerodrome. Although continually under mortar and shell fire. The Germans were now about 600 yds away.

10th

Beginning at dawn, a terrific barrage was put down on the German positions by the Royal Artillery, which continued for four hours. A tank battle began and lasted all the remainder of the morning and afternoon. The Germans were then found to be in full retreat on a six mile front. X Company Scots Guards did not move forward but were ordered to rest.

11th

Very quiet. The enemy were still in full retreat. We began to move from our forward positions to Bayeux for the purpose of resting.

Resting one mile south-west of Bayeux.

12th - 18th

We moved off at 0200 hrs to be part of General Montgomery's drive from Caen to Vimont. We took up our positions about two miles south east of Caen at dawn, waiting for the word go. At 0600 hrs, a gigantic bombardment of the villages to our front was started by the RAF and American Air Force. These villages would have had to have been either captured or by-passed during our advance.

Three of our bombers were shot down in flames. At 0945 hrs the planes stopped their bombardment, but a heavy artillery barrage was put up by the Royal Artillery. At 1200 hrs we began to move forward. We didn't meet any opposition until we reached the village of Cagny, which was captured by X Company and a company of Irish Guards. The village was then surrounded by the Battalion at 2230 hrs. We took up a defensive position for the remainder of the night.

19th

We were ordered to remain in a defensive position forward of Cagny until further orders. The break-through at Vimont was not successful. We only got part way, when our tanks met with a screen of anti-tank guns. We were under constant attack. With this and the snipers, there were many fatalities.

20th

We were still in the same position. No.14 Platoon of X Company was ordered to send forward (about 200 yds) a standing patrol. This was requested for the purpose of observing. I was a member of No.1

section and we were ordered to go first. We arrived at the position. Two of the company's four snipers, Guardsman Dinsdale and Guardsman Jardine, were sent forward another twenty yards to snipe.

At 0800 hrs, Guardsman Jardine was killed by a German sniper. Guardsman Dinsdale received a severe leg wound from an exploding German tank shell. Bullets were now flying all around us. Later, we were relieved by No. 2 section. We returned to the company position. We were constantly shelled, mortared, and sniped at for the remainder of the day. Many more were wounded and killed. The torrential rain made things very difficult.

21st

The standing patrols were still being sent out during the day and still by sections. It was very quiet although we were expecting an attack. It came at 1400 hrs. We were strafed, bombed and machine gunned for about ten minutes by fighter planes. We didn't sustain any injuries this time. It was still pouring with rain and I remember thinking that I had been soaked to the skin for twenty four hours. The roads were thick with mud and the tanks were at a standstill. We were again mortared and shelled during the evening, only this time we sustained more casualties.

22nd

Very quiet all day. Our position was taken over by the Black Watch at 2215 hrs. It had now stopped raining and we began to march along the muddy roads to the rear of our lines. We were still marching at midnight.

23rd

We arrived about two miles south of Caen at 0230 hrs, after a march of four miles, ankle deep in mud. We rested at this position throughout the next three days.

25th

Bombed during the night by enemy planes.

27th

Our orders to move were cancelled.

29th

Still resting two miles east of Caen. We've now been informed, that the reason we are resting in this position is because we are in full view of the enemy. They had to keep their crack Panzer Division on the opposite hill, thus not being able to move them to assist against the Americans at St. Lo.

30th

We moved to a position one mile south of Bayeux. Still resting.

Diary, June 19th - August 12th, 1944. Normandy

31st

We've received orders to move, this time into the Caumont Sector. We travelled in troop carriers for about fifteen miles and then we dug slit trenches to sleep in during the night.

August 1st

We moved off again at 0500 hrs going into the attack. We travelled in troop carriers for the first ten miles and then began marching. Five miles on and the roads became within the range of the German guns and mortars. There were a few casualties to X Company whilst marching along. Corporal Barbour was killed. I remember he was promoted to Corporal in the MT at the same time that I moved from the MT to 14 Platoon.

We marched a further distance of seven and a half miles then formed up to attack, the objective being a hill. The hill was captured in twenty minutes, there was no opposition. We dug in on top of the hill. Later in the day, we moved off again to attack the village of Le Courneur. Once again, there was no opposition, the attack beginning at 2215 hrs and finishing at 2315 hrs. We dug in once again and were ordered to hold the village until dawn when we were informed that tanks would arrive to relieve us.

2nd

The tanks arrived at dawn. The Germans were in full retreat. Reconnaissance units reported the enemy to be twenty miles away. About noon we moved off again and captured the village seven miles away. Once again there was no opposition and we moved on. The purpose being to attack an 88mm gun domineering the road on which we wished to advance.

It was known that there were at least 200 enemy troops in the area of the gun. The attack began at dusk. We reached the objective at about 2300 hrs. Our section of seven men led by Corporal Stevens, spearheaded the attack. We were supported by the remainder of the company, including six or seven tanks. The tanks were ordered to move along the road in convoy and X Company were in the fields to the right and left of the road.

The enemy 88mm gun opened fire at about fifty yards range, knocking out the leading tank. The remaining tanks were ordered to withdraw and orders to X Company were to continue the advance.

At this point, all hell broke loose. About six enemy Machine Gun Posts, opened up together, raking us with fire from front, left and right. There were many casualties. I must admit it was very frightening. Tracer bullets were flying all around; A Guardsman in front of me was shot through the foot. Another, a Sergeant at my right was shot in the heel. I was ordered by Platoon Officer Llewellyn to get the two wounded men back to the stretcher bearers. I succeeded although I was very scared.

Diary, June 19th - August 12th, 1944. Normandy

The battle raged all night and X Company were under continual fire from machine guns. We returned the fire with Bren Guns and rifles. Four Germans were killed for sure and there were many probables.

Another of our men was wounded in the thigh. We were still holding the same position at dawn. The 72 hours continual advance was now held up. We had not slept for the whole time and were beginning to feel exhausted.

3rd

Dawn found us still exchanging shots with the Germans who were only fifty yards to our front. When it was light enough to see we found we were lining a hedge along the side of a farm. The Germans were lining the hedge in front. The hedge was heavily mortared by us and this caused the enemy to return the fire wounding one of our Corporals and killing one of our Guardsmen.

The casualties were now so great, that X Company were very much under strength. Originally there were 135 men in the company and now there were only 90 left.

Suddenly, four Germans moved out of a barn ten yards to the right of our section position, and calmly walked across the farmyard entering a stable. Everyone was too amazed to shoot. We recovered and closed around the stable entrance. Platoon Officer Llewellyn ordered the Germans to surrender and come out of the barn.

The first man emerged in a curious fashion, half crouched. Our suspicions were aroused. Corporal Stevens shot him dead with his Sten Gun. The second German came out in the the same manner. Five rifles cracked, and he fell wounded. One of our Guardsmen noticed him put his hand into his jacket and withdraw a grenade. He shot and killed him. The grenade exploded in his hand.

There were still two more left in the stable. One tried to escape through the rear and he was shot in the neck. He shouted: 'Kamerad'. We took him prisoner. The fourth could not be found. He must have got away through the rear window.

The prisoner turned out to be a Russian, forced to fight by the Germans. He was not very badly wounded.

Snipers began to fire at the slightest movement in our area. I had my narrowest of escapes since arriving in France. Whilst observing over a hedge, instead of through it, a sniper's bullet glanced off the top of my steel helmet.

It was quieter towards evening. The Irish Guards attacked from the left flank after dark, and the Germans retreated through the night.

4th

At dawn, it was very quiet indeed. Occasional shots were fired by a few snipers left behind, but we

Diary, June 19th - August 12th, 1944. Normandy

moved forward again. Once more on the attack, X Company had now been 96 hours without sleep and were very tired indeed. The attack commenced in daylight beginning at 1500 hrs. The objective this time? A farm on an overlooking hill. It was about a mile and a half away.

The advance was held up by four German tanks at the top of the road leading up the hill, two of them being knocked out by our own Sherman tanks. X Company, were ordered to enter the fields on the right of the road to try and bypass the remaining two tanks. The bypass was successful, but we were attacked by machine gun fire from a nearby farm. The two remaining German tanks were now sandwiched with X Company at their front and the Shermans at their rear.

The German tank Commander decided to make a run for it. But he was met by Sergeant Tessler, manning a Piat Gun. The first tank broke through and Sergeant Tessler was killed. The second tank crew evidently, were surprised to find us in the rear for they abandoned the tank. It was captured by us. Intact.

After capturing the farm from where the gunfire that had delayed us earlier, had come from, we dug in and prepared for a counter attack. When it materialised, the enemy were repulsed at dusk, sadly along with the loss of Guardsman McPhee. Two more were slightly wounded. Intermittent firing went on throughout the night.

5th
At 0200 hrs, the 17 pounder guns were brought into position alongside our platoon. Two enemy tanks were knocked out by 0300 hrs, another by dawn. The enemy was retreating again.

We managed to get three hours sleep in the morning and two hours in the afternoon. We were now waiting for orders while resting. At 1945 hrs, orders were received once again, telling us to advance. They stated that we were to advance until fired on, then dig in and hold our position. This we did after only a mile and a half. Night fell with only a few sniper shots and a little mortaring.

6th
Very quiet. The enemy was once again retreating at full speed. We were able to get some sleep during the day. Our position was the same as the previous night's, but we were dug in on the side of the road.

7th
We were still resting although we were getting shelled and mortared all the time. X Company had now been in action for seven days continually. Fortunately we were able to get some rest. The afternoon was very quiet. We were still awaiting orders. The village of Estry was one and a half miles along the road which we flanked.

Diary, June 19th - August 12th, 1944. Normandy

8th

At 1030 hrs. The 15th Scottish Division moved through our lines to go into the attack. At 1200 hrs, many wounded were being moved back and we understood that they had suffered a very tough time at the village of Estry. Our positions were heavily shelled during the morning and afternoon, but we suffered no more casualties. We got some more much needed sleep and the company was beginning to feel less fatigued.

9th

At dawn, we were ordered to prepare to move, but we were still waiting at 1200 hrs. We were shelled all day and at 2100 hrs, we finally began moving. Marching towards the rear of the lines, we were met by troop-carrying lorries and then driven about ten miles east, where once again, we began to march another six miles, the last two being uphill. We were informed that we were approaching the enemy.

10th

At 0230 hrs we arrived at our destination. Two miles east of Vire. We stood by until dawn. We found we were on the slope of a big hill with the enemy on the opposite slope. At 0900 hrs shelling and mortar-fire began by both sides. At 1200 hrs I was hit by shrapnel from an exploding German shell and removed to hospital.

11th

I was in hospital at Bayeux.

12th

A Dakota flew me and other wounded Guardsmen to England. We arrived at Oxford Aerodrome at 1200 hrs."

R. Angus. 2697250. ORPINGTON. KENT.

The Night Patrol, Perugia, Italy - 1943/44.

"These patrols were never sought after, and you hoped you never got them. They were fraught with danger, going forward into No Man's Land with curses and prayers to bring you good luck, which you needed at all times. Captain Toller had once again drawn the short straw for 16 Platoon. It was getting to be a bad habit; this was the second time in six days. We were now under strength, down to fifteen men after taking quite a few losses of late. Our average age was twenty one. Although young and fit, we were fed up with all the fighting, shortage of good hot meals, and lack of bathing facilities. How we used to dream of a soak in a steaming hot bath.

Our objective was the removal of a German observation post two miles to the front of our bogged down position. At dusk we left in single file down the slope, to reach the river and railway track half a mile away. There were constant flares, mortar fire, and the usual spandau cross fire.

On reaching the river without mishap, we found that we could cross by wading up to our waists in the very cold, sluggish, muddy water. Our weapons consisted of grenades and small arms, which enabled us to move faster, when and if, we needed to.

The river crossed, now the rail track, where a wrecked engine and four coaches stood. Toller wanted us to check the coaches to see if they were occupied. This we did, by splitting into threes, and searching one coach at a time, the darkness helping us to dispose of seven Germans, but sadly losing three of our own men.

Having had a breather we found that one of our men needed some first aid for a leg wound. We left him in one of the coaches as he couldn't walk, telling him that we would collect him on the way back. We left in extended line.

Slowly moving forward up the steep but rocky slope, increased mortar fire and flares made the going very hard and sticky. On nearly reaching the hilltop, we split up. Left and right flanks, and Toller and myself dead centre.

We synchronised our watches. In twenty minutes, Toller would fire a flare, then we were all to move in. With a few grenades and hardly any small arms fire we claimed our objective, but paid the price with another four losses. Six Germans also lay dead.

Our instructions on taking the position were to hold it, and then move out at early light. We radioed back our observations on the movements of enemy troops and tanks. With the help of German flares, we saw a lot more than we cared to see. We realised that we would have to be very lucky indeed to stay here safely until daylight. After managing to sweat it out under heavy mortar fire for a while, Toller decided that it would be wiser if we didn't stay as our numbers now totalled only seven.

On the point of moving off and once again looking to my front, there laid on the ground was a three foot sword, with tassels on a red and black

The Night Patrol, Perugia

hand guard. Toller, noticing my interest in the sword called out: "Don't touch that bloody thing Taylor 'till I get out of here," always thinking of booby traps which had cost the platoon so much loss of life.

After prodding around with my bayonet, I assured Toller that it was safe, and I picked up my prize. It was a beauty, a little dirty but I could see no rust. Captain Toller shouted: "Right Taylor, let's be off." We moved out. A few Germans had moved in behind us, but our Company's gunfire was keeping them occupied, my new found weapon claiming one as we made a dash for it.

It's frightening to think that actions which almost come instinctively in a time of war, would almost certainly sicken you at any other time.

On reaching our Company with the loss of two more men, killed I think by our own Company fire, I stuck my blade into the mud banking. I crouched down to get my breath back as I watched it swinging about. Then low and behold, an upstart Major swaggered up, pulled it out of the ground and claimed it for his own. He buggered off with it . Captain Toller seeing the look on my face said: "Never mind Taylor, you might get a medal for this patrol." I didn't get that either."

**N. (BOB) TAYLOR.
ELLAND.
W. YORKS.**

The Bridge

"The sky was leaden, a threatening grey, and the wind was bitterly cold. The ground was frozen solid making my position in the slit trench even more uncomfortable. I did not want to be here but circumstances demanded that I should occupy this dirty, smelly hole in the ground.

My hands were frozen and I could hardly grip my rifle as I peered into the darkness. My hole in the ground was situated in a small wood just outside Arnhem, and the Germans were attacking in force, sending their shells and shrapnel uncomfortably close to our area. I had been here for days just hoping that the enemy would go away and leave us alone.

The shrapnel was getting closer all the time and I wandered if it was only a question of time before we were hit. It was then I heard a shout: "Sergeant Edgeley come here." It was the voice of my superior Officer, Captain J.M. Spencer-Smith. I became panic-stricken realising that if I got out of the trench, I could be decapitated at any time with all the shrapnel flying about. My heart was pounding as I replied: "Coming Sir."

I then dragged my unwilling legs over the side of the trench, and made my way in complete darkness, in the direction of the voice. I wondered just what the hell he wanted. I soon found out, for I had no sooner jumped into his trench, when he growled at me, to take two German SS prisoners

The Bridge

over the bridge for interrogation. He thrust a map in my hand with the directions on. What he didn't mention was that at this time, the bridge concerned was receiving the attention of the German bombers and any such crossing appeared suicidal.

However, there was nothing I could do, other than comply, and I reluctantly put the two pathetic prisoners in the back of the truck. They were bound hand and foot. My eyes were half closed as I put my foot down hard on the accelerator. The bridge was indeed, in a state of chaos, and there were gaping holes all over the place. My truck was hit several times and my windscreen was blown away. I suddenly thought of my family, and what it was going to be like in the next world. I really thought I was dead.

I even started to hum a tune well known to me "Stormy Weather". In fact, I really did not know what the hell I was doing.

Almost mechanically, I found the interrogation centre and handed the prisoners over to the authorities. I suddenly realised that I had to make the return journey. I started praying for God to help me. He did just that. Amazingly a message had come through stating that I was to remain at the centre until things had cooled down. I did not sleep well that particular night, but at least I was safe in my bomb proofed shelter and I was grateful for that."

**MR. E.A. EDGELEY.
SANDBACH.**

Army Cadet Force, Shorncliffe, Kent - 14th August 1960.

*Prince Philip
awarding Long
Service Good
Conduct medal to
E.A. Edgeley
- 1958.*

Always At Risk

"During the Second World War, Private George Wilson diced with death many times in a fantastic series of adventures which would sound fictional were it not for the medals he so proudly owns.

For George, the War began when he was called up to fight on Sept. 2nd, 1939 at the age of 18. He fought in France with the 8th Battalion of the Lancashire Fusiliers and by the time the Dunkirk catastrophe erupted, five of George's close comrades were dead.

Taken prisoner by the Germans his real adventures began, and he was not to see England again for five years.

Packed off in a cattle truck with wounded and dying comrades, he was taken eastward across France. He escaped from the train at the first available opportunity, but was recaptured soon after when French Police swooped while he was hiding out on a farm.

He was shipped eastward once again, to a fort in Poland, where the beds consisted of straw, and food was a loaf of bread amongst three men every four days.

A succession of different camps followed and that winter, he made escape bid after escape bid, crawling out through the wire or disappearing while on working parties. He hated life behind the wire and the inhuman treatment meted out to the inmates. He resolved to make his way across Poland to freedom. Each time he was picked up and condemned to long spells of solitary confinement.

His last escape bid met with success. He was imprisoned in a camp near Danzig and on regular working parties he spied a Russian plane, which landed frequently at a heavily guarded airport.

He spent a fortnight hiding around the hangars waiting for an opportunity to board the plane and escape to Russia.

Giving this up as futile, the guards were too numerous, he threw in his lot with a party of drunken Swedish seamen and boarded their ship in the harbour. He approached the English speaking Captain in the hope that he would help him. But, as the Germans would search the neutral ship before sailing, George was forced to disembark. The Captain had contacts with the Polish underground and the British soldier was handed over to resistance workers.

"I was taken to a house in the city, interrogated and asked if I was willing to join them" said George. "I knew I would never be able to get back to England on my own, so I said yes."

The next three years constituted a saga of a heroic fight against the Nazi oppressors with sabotage the name of the game. George aided his Polish comrades to spike the guns of the invaders.

He was trained in the use of explosives. Troop trains, ammunition and petrol dumps all went up in flames, with the Resistance launching machine gun attacks on the enemy. We didn't stay anywhere long." said George, "We hid out on farms, on barges on the Vistula and we also slept rough in the Black Forest."

He had some close calls and many of his comrades were killed in shoot-outs with the Nazis. Capture and death were never far away, such as the time George and his comrades entered a quiet village, only to be stunned by the sight of armoured cars, tanks and troops thundering down the village street.

"Some building was going on in the village and we picked up shovels and pretended to be workmen. We thought we had been betrayed, but the soldiers were only on manoeuvres fortunately."

Twice in 1943 he and several comrades went behind the wire of a POW camp in a bid to get British and French prisoners to join the war of resistance. He explained: "I told them I was a British soldier and explained my background, but they were afraid it was a trick by the Germans. They were too cagey."

By 1944, Warsaw had become the centre of the national revolt against the Nazis and in August the uprising of the people began. George and his comrades were in the thick of it, fighting amid the ruins of the city.

"We never knew what each day would bring." he said. "And whether we would survive. The Polish people helped us with food and shelter, and in turn we helped the Jews, who also joined in the uprising.

We fought with everything we could lay our hands on."

The shattered city of Warsaw, was the dramatic background to their struggle. By the time of the uprising seventy per cent of the city was in ruins.

By this time, the Russians were only twenty miles outside the city. Events hung in balance, and then George and his comrades were captured. Interrogated by the Gestapo they were denounced as spies and condemned to death.

The worst moment of George's yet action-packed life came when he was tied to a post, blindfolded and forced to face a firing squad. With him were Polish comrades and a fellow British soldier, who had joined the Resistance.

"I really thought we'd had it," he explained, "there was no way out for us." Then a German Officer intervened and called the execution off. He demanded that the two Britons be taken to headquarters for further interrogation.

Travelling through the ruins aboard a lorry, George and his comrade made a bid for freedom. "We knocked the guards out and ran off. In those days I was pretty fit and we outpaced them."

There was nowhere to run to, but into the hands of the Communist invaders: uneasy allies, and where the Poles were concerned they were hardly liberators. The two made their way towards the sounds of battle, through the enemy lines.

"The Russian General was a decent bloke, but

Always At Risk

he gave us two choices: Go into a Russian labour camp or fight the enemy." Well anything was better than going back behind the wire, so they put on Russian uniforms and fought.

Warsaw fell to the Russian advances and the two comrades continued through Poland, pushing the Nazis back to their last stronghold...Berlin.

His comrade (Smith) was bayonetted and put out of action but George, dubbed 'Tommy' by his Russian comrades, pressed on to the crumbling German capital until the Germans surrendered in April, 1945.

He had been with the Russians for nine months. His commander presented him with two medals, thanked him for his support and he was then sent to his original overlords: the British Army.

He was questioned by the Military Police and his story and adventures were duly noted and then he was sent back home to England to his parents. They had had no news of their young son since his capture four years earlier."

GEORGE WILSON.
URMSTON.
MANCHESTER.

A longer version of this extract appeared in the 'Stretford & Urmston Journal'.

The Invasion

"Sunday June 4th, 1944 appeared through the porthole, dull and dour with a choppy sea. We were due to sail at 0900 hrs and the people 'in the know' knew it to be the 'Big D', the invasion of Europe.

It had been the general rumour on board for the past fortnight that the British Higher Authority, with their love of tradition and the help of the sentimental Americans, would choose the Anniversary of Dunkirk for the great event. Since the spring of 1943, it had been expected and anxiously awaited by everybody in the forces, mainly I think, because it heralded a definite view of the end of the road and a return to 'Civvy Street'.

However, when the cable party had all been mustered on the fo'castle, and everyone was reconciled to the endurance of cramped quarters, corned beef meals and Action Stations for the rest of the day, a hand message came aboard from a motor boat announcing that sailing was to be postponed for twenty four hours.

Was it to be Divisions? After all the preparations for sea, no one was in the mood to change into No.1s and parade on the upper deck and stand around like stuffed dummies for the Captain's Inspection. Great was the relief when it was announced as a normal day's routine. The skipper was going to let us in on some of the doings we were to take part in and this he did at 1130, speaking from the flagdeck to the assembled throng below.

The Invasion

In true Nelson fashion, he complimented the ship's company on the cleanliness of the mess decks as noted by him the day before on his Saturday morning rounds. With the remark: "Keep it up", he changed abruptly to the business ahead and gave us the guff on the invasion, except for the date and place of landing... we were left in suspense for the rest of the day.

At 0930 hrs the next morning however, the old winch creaked and the anchor was weighed. The whole flotilla sailed down the Solent. Eight Minesweepers, three Dan Laying trawlers and three Motor Launches in grand array. All around, ships were on the move. Some going in our direction and others heading towards Spithead.

The green shore looked particularly beautiful. Just as a flower looks unbelievably beautiful to a soldier in the battlefield, so the old country looked in all her summer garments, as we rounded the Needles and faced the open sea.

All around us, all manner of queer looking shipping milled impatiently, waiting for the minesweepers to give them a lead. Flags fluttered on taut halyards, signal lamps flashed and the ships formed into sweeping formation. At last, the order 'Out Sweeps' was yelled from the bridge as the leader of the flotilla gave the order. The winch on the quarterdeck hummed and the Oropesa Float sped away from the stern on the end of its cable. The 'Otter' and 'Kite' were lowered and the ships

set their course at a steady eight knots. Behind, the mass of shipping formed into a rough convoy, carefully keeping within the limits of the swept area. Several mines exploded in the course of the day, sounding to those below decks like the clanging of a huge hammer on the ship's side.

As twilight approached, the ship narrowly missed striking a floating mine. But for the good eyesight of a lookout, a slight deviation and a warning signal to the vessels astern, there might have been a big bang. As it was, we carried on as before, after making the necessary adjustments.

When the Isle of Wight had disappeared over the horizon all ships hoisted 'Battle Ensigns' at the masthead in anticipation of enemy opposition. The sight of our red, white and blue bunting flying above us in addition to our normal Ensign abaft the funnel, gave most of the crew that uneasy feeling in the pit of the stomach. What would the next few hours bring?

Pictures of dive bombers, U-Boats and enemy surface craft loomed up in the imagination. Old hands yarned in excited tones of Narvik, Crete or and clash with 'Jerry' that occurred to them. An air of tension and expectancy settled on all. Our doubts and fears were soon swept aside, however, when the French Coast was sighted at about 2200hrs. Towards midnight, hundreds of our bombers passed over, wave upon wave. Formation upon formation. One almost felt like cheering as they carried out

The Invasion

their deadly work. Flashes lit up the skyline and the thunder of exploding bombs came drifting across the sea.

In the course of our voyage, the Captain had spoken over the ship's radio, explaining the when and where of the invasion. The Cherbourg Peninsula was the present objective and as the bombers still came in never ending streams, one wondered if any thing could be left living on that promontory. Eventually, the sky cleared and silence settled in once more. The sweepers swept on.

As soon as an anchorage had been swept off the coast of the peninsula, dark shapes appeared which we presently found to be British Cruisers and Battleships with accompanying destroyers. When in position with engines stopped, they waited with guns pointing ominously towards the shore. It was now about 0500 hrs on the morning of the 6th June and the first troops were due to land at 0700 hrs towards 0730.

'Orion' opened fire, to be followed by 'Ajax' and others. Single shots and broadsides followed fast and furious. Le Havre and Caen were believed to be their targets. Then the landing craft passed us but we didn't see what was happening ashore because we were a few miles out at sea.

Later, the massive concrete boxes of 'Caissons' were towed across the Channel to form the 'Mulberry Harbour' so that tanks, lorries and all manner of equipment could land. A remarkable achievement.

The invasion had taken place. We went on sweeping."

**PETER H. McCREADY.
LITTLETON.
CHESTER.**

H.M.S. Hound - 1946

1945

CHAPTER 8

"At last we were on our way. The previous night we had lain on a beach on the Indian coast waiting to board the Royal Navy ships for our first combined operations. Now, we were sitting below decks approaching Ramree Island, which had been held by the Japs since the early part of the War. As we neared the island, the sound of planes and guns grew louder. We all seemed to stiffen up, but the guts were still there because the grins were still on their faces. I suppose a bit forced, just as mine was.

We belonged to the 36th. LAA Rgt. and our lot was A Troop of the 97th Battery; we had been in and out of Burma for the last two years. One of our Officers must have noticed the tension because he disappeared up the ladder. After a few minutes, he returned and told us to split our group in half and then for one half to go up to the upper deck for some fresh air.

I thought then that it wasn't the state of the air he was worried about. It was more our nerves. However, the fresh air did the trick. We all felt a great deal better for it.

As we got our first look at the island, I wondered what was in store for me. Fighter Bombers were diving over the island bombing and machine gunning. Two destroyers were bombarding the beaches with shells. Further inland, one solitary gun was replying to the fire of the destroyers. It was a cat and mouse game between them. As the shells from shore dropped near the ships, the ships moved further out, and as the Japs got the range again, they moved further in.

Suddenly we were ordered below decks, and I thought to myself: "This is it." Then, the Officer's voice on the tannoy system told us to get ready. As I gulped the air down, and it seemed I couldn't get enough of it, I started to fix my gear on. I couldn't manage it so I helped one of my mates on with his, and he, with mine.

An Officer's voice spoke again, telling us what was going to happen. Actually, we had already been briefed for the job, but he said he would let us know how the landings were going. I will never forget his voice as we sat there; it was cool. Cooler than that of a commentator at a race meeting.

The Lincolns and Green Howards were making the first landings if my memory serves me right, and my mob was to follow in as second line infantry, to hold the beach until our guns, the bofors, came ashore.

The Officer began to describe the landings, saying: the Lincolns are nearing the beach, and now they are scrambling ashore and every man is still on his feet. I took a deep breath and exclaimed: the Lincolns are over the first barrier and every man is still on his feet. Now they are spreading out, in and moving forward. I don't know how it happened, but all the lads around me gave quiet hurrahs at the same time.

Then suddenly, what we had been waiting for happened. Over the tannoy came the shout: "Up on deck A troop." The next minute, we were climbing down the nets into the assault craft and making our way to the shore. There were six craft in line, and ours was first. As our craft approached the island, the petty Officer in charge was looking back, and noticed a naval Officer sending a message in semaphore. As he couldn't read it, he asked the AB on the wheel if he could read it for him.

"OK, PO", he answered, "I'll have to turn the boat about so that I can see." "OK", said the PO "come about then, and afterwards, fall back in line behind the second boat."

While this was happening my job was to watch the skies for Jap planes. When the message was read, the craft turned and fell back into line, heading once again, towards the shore. Apparently, the message was only a joke from one of the Officers on board, to our own Officer. They had become friendly. His reply was a smile, and a V sign directed back towards the ship.

At the same time, a corvette was approaching; she was to cross the bows of the first assault craft, which actually should have been us. The next second, there was a bright flash and a terrific roar. Turning my head, all I could see was the bows of the corvette sinking back under the water. There was no sign of the assault craft. Everything had disappeared, including the men. All I could think of was, that if it wasn't for that signal from the ship, then it would have been us. It was no consolation to the men who perished.

Nobody spoke as we sailed over the spot where the craft had disappeared. We looked hopefully into the water for somebody to rescue. There was no sign of life at all, and we weren't allowed to stop.

We hit the beach, waded ashore and took cover behind a five feet high mud wall. Stretched out along the wall was a mixture of Frontier Force, Rifles, and Gurkhas. The British troops were ready to hold the beach if the Japs counter-attacked.

As we sat there, a Scottish Sergeant belonging to one of our guns came across to give us a pep talk. He stood there telling us what we were going to do to the little so and so's. He kept chasing away flies and mosquitoes from his neck. He was about six feet in height, and he towered over the wall we were sheltering behind. I sat beside two of my pals, Eddie Cahill from Newcastle, my home town, and an Irish lad by the name of Mickey. We were on the beer together whenever there was any. We'd been together since 1941 and it was now April or May of 1945.

The Sergeant kept talking and cursing the flies and mosquitoes. A Gurkha came across, bent over, and tapped our Sergeant on the back saying: "Sahib. Nay mosquito. Japany wallah Bonduk." He then pointed his finger across the area where the Jap

was. Well, the Sergeant just fell flat and looked at us. We burst out laughing, as we couldn't help it. What he thought was flies and the like, was a Jap sniper. After a few minutes, he crawled away. I'm sure he went to change his pants.

Further along, I noticed a Gurkha, Havilda, speaking to a couple of his men, who promptly drew their kukris, put them in their mouths, and crawled off. One of our lads murmured: "bye, bye Jap." Sure enough, about one hour later, they crawled back, grinned at us, and drew their fingers over their throats.

Some of the Japs had buried themselves in small trenches, covered over by the Japs, and left there. Some of the Lincolns must have actually walked over them as they advanced forward. When the Lincolns were well forward, the Japs lifted their heads and began sniping at us.

Later on in the afternoon, we heard a faint drone in the sky. One of our lads pointed to an airplane about 20,000 - 30,000 feet up. We couldn't identify it until we heard the faint noise of machine guns. Above the plane was a smaller one, and they were having a go at it until a black object fell suddenly from the larger plane. The plane itself began falling, going around and around like a falling leaf. We then saw the markings. It was a Jap plane, and over it a Spitfire did a victory roll. At once, the launch went out before the plane ever hit the water and brought the Jap pilot ashore. He was still alive,

The Sun is Setting

but died later. The black object we had seen falling away was the engine, which had broken away from the plane after the Spitty had blasted it.

Eventually, our guns came ashore. Bofors, 25 pounders and the vehicles. We took over our gun to revert to our normal role of anti-aircraft, and our bofors were fully mobile, as the gun was built onto the chassis of a truck and did not have to be towed. Its speed was reckoned to be about 40 mph, and I know that on one occasion it went faster than that on the Burmese mainland.

We were given orders, and off we went, following a small narrow track hammed on by trees. The track was about as wide as the span or width of our wheels, and we were watching every bush, ready to shoot. To the right of the track we saw a Jap bunker. There was only one thing to do-reconnoitre - and so we did. We found that it was empty but we didn't go in as the Japs were too handy with booby traps. Travelling a bit further, we selected our gun site and settled in for the night.

The following morning, more shocks were in store for us. As we were standing at dawn with the light just breaking through, our eyes were glued on every tree and bush to our right. About three hundred yards away was the sea. Suddenly, one of our lads, by the name of Barfoot said: "What's that down by the water's edge?" We all crouched as we looked. It could have been logs, or it may have been Japs who had come ashore during the darkness.

After a while, our Sergeant, who had been a gunner with us said: "Let's have a look." We found what was left of the lads who had been blown up in front of us the previous day.

After reporting our findings to HQ we took their belongings from them, paybooks, etc., including any personal ones. One of them had a letter from his mother, asking why he wasn't being sent home as he was six months overdue on his expat. I thought then that this poor fellow wouldn't be going home, and somehow, I thought Blighty is a long way away, if I ever reached it.

Later that morning, as we sat around the gunpit scrounging dog-ends off each other, several blokes came through the bushes toward us. We noticed they were Sappers looking for any traps the Japs had left behind. The Corporal in charge came across and asked us how we had gotten here. Straight along the track and turned off into the bushes across here. Two or three of us went back with them to the same pathway we had travelled on the previous night. The NCO asked: "Did you pass this spot?" We told him we had, so he took us about two or three yards off the track and pulled us to one side. We were speechless, as standing on its base was a 500lb bomb. That, said the Corporal, was wired up with the detonator right in the middle of the road. How did you miss setting it off? We all realized then that it was only because we were riding on the bus that we had been saved. If that

The Sun is Setting

pathway had been wider, one of our wheels would have set off that detonator.

After that things became quieter. The Japs were driven to the north of the island. Every night, they tried to escape by small boats to the mainland, but the Royal Navy's patrol boats generally caught them. If they made a fight of it, that was their bad luck.

At night time as we lay in our slit trenches, we could hear the Japs shouting, yelling, and screaming. We thought they were trying to wear our nerves our in readiness for an attack on our lines which had them cut off from the rest of the island.

It was later when we got to the north of the island that we came across the remains of Japs who had been attacked by crocodiles who had come out of the swamps and dragged them in terror screaming back into the darkness of the swamps. That was the screaming we had heard.

The days rolled by, and the 25 pounder crews were brought back to the centre of the island to dig in and rest. Our job was to guard them from any Jap planes. These generally came over at night in ones and twos. A Jap came across flying very low, trying his usual tricks. An idea must have struck him. It was a moonlit night, and he probably saw the native village in our area. The so and so attacked it, and sent it up in flames. It lit up the surrounding area, and we could see him plain as daylight repeatedly diving in low. We decided to have a bash because he was flying low over the 25 pounders.

Waiting until he passed our crossing point, we let him have it. We missed, but he turned and made the same run. Crossing our fingers, we waited until he was between us and the moon, and we had another go at it. I was behind Jack, our gunner driver, who was in No.2 seat, directing his aim by observing the tracer. The Sergeant was behind in No.3, directing him.

It seemed he was going out of range, but during our second last round, the burst got his tail. A great glow of fire spread around him, and he started diving toward the sea, speedily disappearing out of sight behind the trees. It was pats on the back for each other and big grins all around.

The next day, we were credited with the plane from our headquarters and given an official pat on the back. Later that night, some NCOs and gunners from the 25 pounders came across and asked us if it was our gun which had shot down the Jap. We told them it was, and out came a bottle of rum and a few bottles of beer. We had our own ration of beer, and what a night we had.

About 0200hrs that night, the others decided it was time they went back, so our cook, Bill, said he would show them the way. He didn't come back until about 0900hrs the next morning. It appeared he had fallen down in an animal trap set by the natives. So the other fellows took him back to their camp for the night. After that when we asked him to show us the way, we had to duck quickly.

The Sun is Setting

The Sun is Setting

As time went by we got the usual football matches going, until the day a call came from the Air Force for supply dropping to the West Africans on the mainland. I thought I might as well have a go, so about twenty of us each day went up into the Dakotas until the Africans were supplied.

Finally, the day we had been waiting for came. We were going back to India. After that, we didn't know the War wasn't over yet. I think it was either June or July of 1945 when we boarded the transports which were to take us off the island. As I stood by the rails alongside my pals, watching the island receding in the distance, I thought, that's that. What now?"

R.L. CONROY.
GATESHEAD.
TYNE & WEAR.

UNDATED ACCOUNTS

CHAPTER 9

"In my Japanese Prison Camp were seven long prison sheds to house the prisoners, each one divided into sections with rooms at strategic points. Running through each of them was a gangway with the toilets outside at one end. Around the sheds was an electric fence about five feet high with a four feet spread. The rooms were used by senior ratings and civilians, the Officers having their own shed.

Outside our compound was a road and further buildings where the Japanese quarters and the cookhouse were. Behind these was a ten foot high brick wall running all the way around the outside of the camp. On top of this wall was an electric fence. There were also guard towers placed at strategic places along it, manned for twenty four hours a day.

The Japanese Sgt. Major started walking about the camp closely followed by a small chicken. This thing appeared to have a charmed life, for the electric fence was certainly active as the loss of a few prisoners had proven. We named the chicken Pedro. As the days got longer and longer, he began to look better and better. In fact, he looked so good that one day he disappeared.

The Japanese pulled the camp virtually to pieces in their endeavour to find out just who had been responsible for his disappearance, but all they found was a few feathers in such a position as to be unable to lay the blame at anyone's doorstep. I never knew how he was captured, but I did know how he

The Legend of Pedro

tasted, for the senior American civilians in one of the smaller rooms invited me in as a guest to his demise party. Although we did not have the benefit of roast potatoes and brussels sprouts to accompany him, I can assure everyone that he tasted just as good.

The legend of Pedro gave us a good laugh, raised our morale considerably, and became incorporated in our camp songs."

J. MARINER. BOURNEMOUTH. DORSET.

Tribute To Jock Dark

"Jock Dark's end has always been a bit of a mystery. I had the privilege of being 'two man tent mate' with him at the final stages of the War. We were using 'Fuzzy Power,' the 75mm mountain guns. The more they sang, the better they pulled.

On the critical day it was my job to look for a track to pull the gun along the next day. At the time I was ill with malaria. Jock, after cutting tent poles and erecting our joint home, said to me: "You look a bit off colour, I'll go and recce the track." He did not return.

A couple of days later, after getting the gun into position, we fired a few rounds. We went in with the infantry, the 2/5 Battalion, to try and square off for Jock.

All we found was rotten meat and the Japs' dixies. A sad end for a staunch friend."

**ALAN MAXTED.
KIPPAX RING.
QUEENSLAND. AUSTRALIA.**

Kamikaze

"During World War Two, in the Pacific, the newly created British Pacific Fleet began to take part in the great Pacific battles.

The carriers 'Indomitable', 'Indefatigable', 'Victorious', and 'Illustrious', battleships 'King George V' and 'Howe', five cruisers and ten destroyers, took station on March 26th, and began round the clock strikes against the airfields of The Sakashime Islands and Formosa. The British ships were designated Task Force 57.

The Japanese had been using Kamikaze pilots for some time, and had inflicted much damage on American warships. Task Force 57 in later operations were given similar attention. All the carriers mentioned, plus the 'Formidable', which relieved the 'Illustrious' were hit, but were never out of action for more than a few hours. This story concerns a Kamikaze attack on the 'King George V'.

During the engagement, the suicide plane was observed plunging through the heavy flak, towards the 'King George V'. It hit the superstructure near to the Bridge, which became hidden from view by the resultant explosion and smoke.

Almost immediately she re-appeared and from the winking of her signal light, flashed the message: "The Yellow B".

"I hope you are not referring to me", flashed the 'Indomitable' in reply, jokingly. This was quickly followed by a more concerned message: "Have you sustained any damage?" To those of us who could read this silent conversation, the amusing answer from 'King George V' was: "Scratched paintwork."

W. J. BROWN. BOLTON. LANCS.

Wreckage of one of two Kamikazes to hit H.M.S. Indomitable.

Greater Love Hath No Man

A sailor's letter to his mother.

Dear Mum,

"If you ever come to read this, it will be most likely that, I your son Jack will have left this world. I have no premonition or any feeling of getting killed, but this is just in case, and there are a few things that I feel I would like you to know.

Can I express in worlds of words my thanks or my love? I do not think that is possible. I thank you for all the love sympathy and understanding which you have always shown me. I have always been able to lean on you and you have never let me down. You have always helped me with a smile. All I can say is just thank you. I love you just as you love me.

A man in the Services realises more what a mother means to him. You fed me, clothed me, and gave me a comfortable home. Knowing all this perhaps you will understand why I feel happy to be doing my bit for King and Country. Really, it is for all the things you have brought me up to respect. I was born into the world an Englishman, and if I am ever born again, I hope I am an Englishman".

This letter took three years to reach Warrington. It arrived one morning when Jack was at home after being repatriated from Italy. It was simply addressed 'For my mother'. Across the corner was written. "Opened by the Kit Examiner Officer". It was enclosed and directed in an H.M.S. Envelope.

The Voyage

Dear Mum,

"This is a diary of the voyage, me being a mess-man. I'm excused duties (that's going on watch) from 6 o'clock in the morning 'til 8 o'clock in evening. We're in three watches red (mine), white and blue - they're called action watches, I've also been given an Action Station, a Lewis Gun on the Bridge.

The time is 8 o'clock Tuesday, 18th April. We sailed this morning at 9 o' clock. There's a heavy swell running, but she's not rolling much; one chap is sea-sick, so I've had his supper. Taffy's in my watch, that's from 12 o'clock till 4 tomorrow. Seeing that we've got to turn to again at 6 o'clock we won't get any sleep, except for an hour or two before we go on.

9.30 - Taffy and I have just been on the upper deck listening to two chaps playing piano-accordions; it's a warm pitch black night. We've got paravancs (they're for protection against mines) ready on the forecastle, but we haven't run them yet. I'm just going to turn in on the stool; it's not worth slinging a hammock for two hours sleep.

4.15 - Wednesday morning, 19th. Just come off watch, a two hour spell on the bridge, on the engine room telegraphs (but we don't touch them unless there's an accident, or someone falls overboard). When the Quarter-Master wants a smoke or a cup of cocoa, we take the wheel. He stands behind us, just in case. Our course is 110 degrees east and this swell takes some holding her. Taffy relieved me at 2 o'clock. Well I've got to turn to at 0600 and I'm dog tired, so I'm going to crack-it down on one of the stools.

3.15 - Wednesday afternoon, and it's been a grand day. I've just been up on deck, and had my photo taken several times, been sunbathing, it's make and mend (that's a half-day for watches who haven't got the afternoon watch). We're holding some boxing bouts tomorrow night (only exhibitions). I'm sparring with the ships singer, called Bing! The P.T.I. is sparring with Bob Reynolds. We've got the first watch, from 8 'til 12 o'clock on the bridge. It's as calm as a mill pond. The sea is a vivid blue almost purple. We did evolutions today.

12.15 - Thursday morning. Just been relieved on the bridge. We're running paravanes now. We've been singing along to the accordions till 10 o'clock My favourite was requested several times (Let Us Be Sweethearts). Well I think I'll turn in, turn out, turn round and turn too. Just (Taffy did it) knocked the ink all over the deck; she's rolling well now.

8 O'clock - Thursday night, the boxing is postponed; its too rough. We're having evolutions, and darken ship so a couple of blue lights are the only ones on deck, (more barked shins than that). Often the air is the same colour. We've got the morning watch, that's from 4 o'clock till 8 in the morning. Well I think I'll turn in 'til 4 o'clock. This morning watch is the best of the lot. I'm excused the dog watches. We're doing about 11 knots, and I'm told that we'll arrive in Alexandria tomorrow so this is the last night at sea (for a while).

8.15 - Friday morning just come off. It was very foggy at 4, but as the sun came out it lifted. Our speed was reduced to about 6 knots; the sea is dead calm, still haven't seen land yet. Well I've got to dish up and scrub out yet, don't feel like breakfast.

1.30 - Friday afternoon we've arrived. For about a mile along the coast is nothing but sand; in the distance we can see palm trees and buildings. We nearly sank a Dhow; it drifted right into our path. They cursed us north, south, east and west, our ancestors, those that come after us, those before us, upside down, the other way up, inside out, outside in. If their breath had held out they would still be cursing. There's swarms of Egyptians alongside in boats, selling anything.

Well Mum, hang on to this, stow it away somewhere and for the present, Cheerio."

Always your loving son,
Jack.

The Prisoners of Siberia

They came early in the morning to take them by surprise
Dragging out the men and boys, ignoring the women's cries
They were the Russian soldiers with their bayonets and guns
Who came that day and took away their husbands, brothers and sons
The soldiers took them to a wood where they shaved off all their hair
Then took their clothes and gave them prison uniforms to wear.

At the railway station, hungry, cold and damp
They waited for the train to take them to the prison camp
For two days and nights they waited and when at last it came
They were the open cattle trucks carrying prisoners just like them
The guards gave them cabbage soup and black bread the first they'd had to eat
Then herded them into the trucks as if they were herding sheep.

Almost every morning they would find a prisoner dead,
The guards would have him thrown from the truck then shoot him through the head
At night the prisoners huddled close to keep each other warm
The weather got colder and colder, still the train went on and on
The stench on the trucks was putrid from secretions, and urine
And the rotting flesh of frostbite that had turned to gangrene.

The food, when they got it was like pig swill but they ate to stay alive
The question uppermost in their minds was when will we arrive?
The journey so far had taken three months and covered three thousand miles
When they released them from the trucks the guards were full of smiles
They were smiles of satisfaction at the horror and the pain
On the faces of the prisoners as they cuffed them to the chain

They were given warmer clothing soup and bread and boots to wear
They were chained to one another as they set off pair by pair

The Prisoners of Siberia

Fastened to the back of a lorry they walked for twelve hours and then
After only two hours rest they were forced to start again
On they walked for three more days until there was nothing in sight
They walked all day but now, the guards allowed them to rest at night

The blizzards and great falls of snow made it so much harder to tread,
And one by one the weakest of the prisoners dropped dead
These men had walked nine hundred miles and with just nine more miles to tramp
They looked forward to some food and rest as at last they neared the camp
None of them would have ever believed they'd be glad to see this place
Rows upon rows of wooden huts in stark open space

All around for miles and miles on every side was snow
Was this to be their home, then where else was there to go?
Just how long could they survive on what little they were fed?
Working all day from dusk 'til dark on a quarter of a loaf of bread
As these Polish men climbed onto their beds half frozen and in pain
They prayed that one day they would see their families again

Mercifully a lot of them died but some of them lived to tell
The world just what happened when the Russians took them to hell.

"This is a true story of what happened to my husband, and hundreds of other Polish men and boys who were taken forcibly from their homes. He was later liberated by General Sicorski, and joined the British Army after a short recuperation. He joined the 8th Army and served in Syria, then came to live in England in 1946/47.......
He never saw any of his family again."

MRS WLADYLAW WOLONCIEJ.
DONCASTER.
YORKS.

Latrines

Albert Findlow
at Manston
R.A.F. Station
- 1943/44

"I served with the Royal Signals during the War. A funny incident happened to me whilst in Burma with the mobile Kinema section.

We were all Sergeants and it was my turn as orderly dog. One of the duties was to treat the field latrines with D.D.T. The latrines were long deep pits surrounded by a hession and then sub-divided for a little privacy. I had the assistance of a Naik, (an Indian Corporal) who inadvertently, picked up a jerry can of petrol by mistake. This was duly poured into the latrine. On smelling the petrol, I took the precaution of dropping several pieces of lit paper down to burn off the fuel.

Satisfied that everything was now in order, I carried on with other chores. An hour later there was such a boom. One of the Sergeants had gone in to attend to the call of nature, lit a cigarette and flicked the lit match between his legs. Boom! The petrol fumes had not been dispersed and or course they had ignited. Out came the NCO, swearing and cussing, his private parts now hairless. Needless to say, the air was blue."

A. FINDLOW.
MIDDLETON. MANCHESTER.

What's For Dinner

"I was one of a party of 30 POWs who were employed by Kristaleiss Fabrik Und Kuhltransit Aktiengesselschaft in Leipzig in Germany. We were employed in the cold storage where all types of food were stored. This had been seized in Denmark and was to be used to feed the German forces.

The work was extremely hard but the pickings made it worthwhile. As a POW I think we can safely say that food ranks high in priority in the mind. We all knew the penalty if we were caught stealing but this did not deter us a great deal. We were helped in this because of the fact that all the Germans employed with us were also on the same game. Not quite to the extent that the British POWs were. If we had been reported to any of the Germans, the Gestapo would have taken over the cold storage and that would have meant the end of things for the Germans as well. The chief commodities which we dealt with were pork, beef, butter and eggs.

I suppose you could say it was a very cosmopolitan gathering because I think we had POWs from every nation with whom Germany was at War with. This included many Russians whom the German civilians and guards treated abominably. In spite of all these nationalities only the German civilians and the British POWs were allowed to handle the food. I can assure you that we did our best to supply the unfortunates who were not allowed near the food.

I often wonder what the German quarter-master thought when they received frozen pigs with only three legs, or two legs, or one leg and sometimes with no legs at all. Half-full barrels of butter with no sign of a break in the barrel and half-empty crates of eggs with no sign of ever being tampered with.

Where we lived and slept (the lager) there were also two German sentries living with us which made it impossible to cook our ill-gotten gains without their knowledge. They had to be included in our list of customers. The most barefaced thing we achieved was the theft of a complete half pig and a very large one at that. Then managing to get it upstairs to the lager without the sentry seeing it. How this was done is another story. The half pig was then duly installed through the trap door and into the loft of the lager for safe keeping.

The following morning we went to work leaving one man behind. It was his responsibility for cleanliness in the lager. On our return from work that day he told us what had happened. For the first time ever whilst we had been there the Gestapo had made a flying raid to see what they could find. As good as they were they were unable to find anything incriminating. Having given up they were on the point of departure when one of the jack-booted master race espied the trap door to the loft.

Bringing this to the attention of the German Officer who then ordered him to climb up and have

149

W A R · M E M O R I E S

What's For Dinner

a look. Climbing on one of the beds he moved the trap door and poked his head through. The Germans for some reason only looked in one direction and reported to the Officer that there was nothing to be seen whilst behind him in all it's glory was the half pig.'

The Germans then departed without bothering to close the trap door. The POW who was there whilst the search took place was never able to say what his feelings had been. I think that it is safe to say that had that Gestapo Sergeant turned his head only 90 degrees he would have spotted what was up there and I think that 30 POWs would have been unaccountably lost."

**F.L. WALTON. GOOLE.
N. HUMBERSIDE.**

The Hospital

"I was behind Captain Vickers of the East Surrey Regiment when he shot dead a Jap Officer at point blank range. He shouted to me to search the dead man so I rolled him over onto his back.

I found a school map which had our positions marked on it, circled in red ink and a pocket watch which I intended to keep as a souvenir when the War was over. That was a stupid thing to do and it could have cost me my life in the weeks to come.

Jap gunfire set the oil tanks ablaze and the thick smoke began to envelope Singapore. Everything was black by day and a red glow lit up the night sky. Lt. Colonel Varley, C.O. Of the Australian Army said: "I've never experienced such concentrated shell fire over such a period".

All this plus the bombing by Jap planes added to the turmoil. People were starting to panic. The soldiers were trying to push their way through the civilians to get aboard the last boats leaving Singapore. It was only days before capitulation and one of the biggest defeats in the history of the British Army.

During the fighting I was hit in the shoulder. I was also suffering from a seeping ulcer and was looking around for somebody to attend my wound, when a truck appeared carrying Chinese Communist Guerillas. They immediately took me to the Queen Alexandra Hospital and left me at the entrance.

I managed to weave my way past the dead and dying. A doctor told me to go upstairs; this probably saved my life. I saw a medical orderly, Cpl. Sinclair who bandaged my throbbing ulcer, but had to leave the shrapnel in my shoulder.

During the early hours of the morning, I heard the familiar rat-a-tat of Japanese rifle fire. I hobbled to the window and looked out. I saw a Japanese soldier advancing towards the hospital and then all hell broke loose downstairs.

The Japanese had gone beserk bayonetting surgeons and patients. Doctors tried to plead with them but to no avail. They went on killing. Suddenly I remembered the Jap Officer's watch I had. God I thought, if they find me with it, I'll be dead. I hobbled to the toilets where, with great difficulty, I placed the watch on the cistern. I had just got back to my bed when the swing doors flew open. There stood two Japanese soldiers, one over six feet tall and the other about five feet.

They stayed there with fixed bayonets as they looked up and down the ward. In the small Jap's right hand was a squawking duck trying to get free. The tall Jap went up to the first two heavily bandaged soldiers and looked at their wrists for watches. Finding none he proceeded to bayonet them. Cpl. Sinclair then stepped forward with some bread and tea on a tray to try to pacify them but was immediately felled by the butt of a rifle.

Luckily, a Japanese Officer came in and saw what was happening and kicked the soldiers

The Hospital

downstairs. He apologised saying that due to the fighting, his men hadn't eaten for two days. The massacre at the hospital was never given publicity and many are still unaware it ever happened.

After the fall of Singapore, working parties were sent to build the Burma railway, known as the death railway. It was completed in 18 months with men working in atrocious conditions. We were starved and beaten by savage captors who broke all the rules of civilized conduct. Out of the 60,000 POWs working on the railway, 15,000 died.

When it was completed, those regarded as fit (that's if you could stand) were sent to work in Japan. Less than 1,000 of us left Singapore on a tramp steamer. We were hurled down into the hold. Most of us were suffering from malaria, dysentry, beri-beri and malnutrition. It was black and hot down there. We had no water or food. Within a few hours, men began to scream and go mad, so you can imagine the smell and conditions. When men began to die they let some light and fresh air in. After about two days they let us up on deck.

Just past the Phillippines we ran into American subs who were patrolling the South China Sea. Then, after splitting from our convoy, we ran into a typhoon and were shipwrecked off Formosa. Eventually the Jap Navy took us in to Osaka in 1944.

After suffering two and a half years of Jap barbarity, we thought nothing else could happen to us, but it did as the end came quickly when the atom bomb dropped 120 miles away at Hiroshima.

We came home on the Queen Elizabeth in November, 1945, to a government that seemed not to care. We were given a cursory check-up by doctors and paid just £78 from Japanese assets for all our sufferings."

J. WYATT. SYDENHAM. LONDON.

DISTANCE HAS NO MEANING IN THE VAST WASTES OF THE WESTERN DESERT.

"I was a founder member of the world famous 'Desert Rats' and although only a young man, I was looked on as a hard nut 'desert-wise survivor'. It was because of this unwanted name I had, that I was picked out to go back down the line several hundred miles, for spares that we needed urgently. A 'babbies' job you may think, but not so. Facing the enemy in the line was child's play in comparison to this trip. The natural elements of the desert and all the pitfalls one may come across was far greater a threat than any enemy could ever be. One wrong decision on the trip and you were a dead man.

I was told that I could take any two men I wanted, plus any vehicle. I chose my two best mates and a three ton Bedford truck. One of them was a first class motor mechanic, a vital man to have on such a trip, and the other man was very good at putting on a meal with little, or nothing to work with. So far, so good.

You name it, and we put it on our truck. Oil, water, petrol, food, and anything else we thought we may need. We were ready. This trip was going to take well over a week if all went well, for you must remember, 30mph would be our top speed. A long drive with two mates, who were more like brothers. So, off we went on our trip down the line; we couldn't have been more confident. All was going to be alright.

Our driving day would be a full 12 hours, from sunrise to sunset and you would think that on such a trip, you would see lots of troops. Not so. You could travel for days and not see a solitary soul. We spent our days telling jokes, singing, and small talk. Anything to break the boredom of the long drive.

It was on just such a day when we saw a small one ton pick-up coming towards us. As it came closer, we called out to the driver to stop. On board were four RAF Officers. We all climbed out of our vehicles. Three young 'Desert Rats', battle hardened as young as we were, and four higher ranking RAF Officers.

Their driver didn't see the point as to why we should stop them, but we were struck with horror when we saw how green these young men were and the lack of vital equipment and supplies. They may have just been going up the M62 to Blackpool, rather than going across the murderous wastes of the Western Desert. They told us that they were on their way to an airfield several hundred miles away.

Although we were out-ranked, their was no doubt about it, we just had to take charge of the situation. If these four men were going to make it to their airfield alive, they were going to need a great deal of help to get there.

We loaded their truck with all the oil, water,

The Desert Rat

Fred Gibson (centre) with friends, on leave in Cairo, before the big battle.

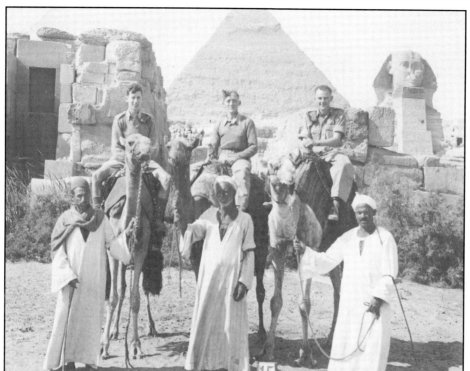

food, and anything else we could spare (including ammunition) just in case. By this time our cook had prepared an appetizing, two course meal. The RAF. lads got stuck in to it like a pack of hungry wolves. It was the best meal they had tasted since they had arrived overseas they said. We went on to stress the pitfalls that could lay ahead, without frightening them in any way. This was very important.

The time soon came when we had to say our goodbyes, and it was at this point the RAF driver asked us if he could get more supplies ahead. This is the point that I want to make about distance having no meaning. "Yes", we all said, "you're in luck, there is one just a few miles down the road. Keep following it until you come to the bend, and then you will find it, ten miles further on." The RAF men left to find their airfield, we to collect our supplies.

The three of us felt great. We had done our good deed for the day, and saved four good young men from almost certain death. Then a terrible thought struck us, yes, the supply point was back where we said it was. The only trouble was, that we had passed it four days ago.

I sure hope to God these young men made it to their airfield, for they are always on my mind."

**FRED GIBSON.
STRETFORD. M/C.
EX Desert Rat 7th Armoured Div. 8th Army.**

Out of Bounds

I've fought beneath a scorching sun
On sandy battle grounds
Though many times a town is won
It's always 'out of bounds'

Though NCOs and privates too
Lie dead 'neath sandy mounds
The only place and this is true
That's never out of bounds

Every rank in battle dress
To Sergeant Majors crown
Never use each others mess
Because its out of bounds

And when in town on well earned leave
To spend your hard earned pounds
Unless you've tapes on your sleeve
The best shows out of bounds

I've fought for Britain and Her cause
On democratic grounds
But sad to say it's here I pause
For England's out of bounds

Each and all a mother's son
That fights 'til victory sounds
Grant the same to all and one
And banish out of bounds

Sent in by Mrs Margaret Corkill.

**Written by
her late husband whilst serving in
the 67th Green Howard,
Yorkshire Rgt.
8th Army, in North Africa.**

A War Remembered

" H.M.B.Y.M.S. 218

Having qualified as a gunlayer at Whale Island and Chatham, I was sent back to my depot at Lowestoft where soon after, I was drafted to places unknown.

We boarded the troopship 'Empress of Scotland' at Greenock. We sailed alone finding ourselves in Halifax N.S. Canada, seven days later. We left there by train and away we went across the mighty continent of North America.

After a brief stop in Montreal, we were soon speeding across the Rocky Mountains. Fitted to the front of the powerful steam train was a snow plough. It was exciting to watch the snow being piled high on both sides of the track.

The scenery was magnificent and we hardened War Veterans were like a load of school children on an outing. In fact, at one stop we made, St Albans, the train swiftly emptied as everyone rushed over to the brightly lit street, and with the kindness of the people, we changed money and bought anything and everything just at the sheer delight of the lights and all the goodies on display.

The train was delayed for an hour whilst the Officers rounded us all up. The journey to the U.S. took three days and two nights. It was a very brief glimpse of New York and then we arrived at our destination - Asbury Park, New Jersey.

The Navy had taken over two large hotels in the sea front, erected railings and called the whole complex HMS Asbury. This was now a receiving and holding barracks for crews awaiting ships, yet to be built. I was to spend three weeks here and very nice it was too.

The American people were most hospitable. Families would wait outside the gates in their huge cars and invite us to their homes for dinner. They were really wonderful to us.

The U.S. Servicemen were tolerant of us, but many skirmishes took place. I suppose it was much the same attitude back home in the U.K. Their forces were overpaid and over there, whilst we were over in the States, and very underpaid. We found ourselves very popular. Free drinks in the bars, etc., so it was inevitable that fights would break out now and then. Nothing serious though. After all, we were all on the same side in this War. All fighting to free the world from oppression.

Came the day that my name appeared on the notice board to join a ship now at Brooklyn Navy Yard some ninety miles from Asbury. I left, along with a bunch of men who were to be my comrades in arms, and very dear shipmates over the next three and a half years.

A coach took us and dumped us outside the Fulton Gate entrance to the navy yard. No one was in charge. No one met us. All the Officers and senior rates were already on board. Which ship and where was still a mystery to us. Nobody knew.

For some unknown reason they nominated me to find out where we were supposed to be. I approached the U.S. sentry and inquired as to the whereabouts of the minesweepers which were expecting crews. He directed me to a building to where the 'limey' Officers were.

This proving successful, we were directed to one of the piers where our ship was berthed. It was the U.S.Y.M.S. 188. We straggled along, dragging our gear and we eventually found our new home. An Officer was at the bridge watching this motley crowd arrive, swarming all over the gangway. It was our C.O. Skipper. Lt. Richard Hannaford RNR. and did I detect a raised eyebrow at the sight of us?

The coxswain, CPO Charlie Manthorpe met us and directed us below, saying that bunks had been allocated, and that there was a not meal ready. At last we were home. The family was ready to be moulded.

The following morning the crew were assembled on the after deck and prayers were said. The Stars and Stripes were lowered, to be replaced by the White Ensign of the Royal Navy. We were now, H.M.B.Y.M.S. 2188. A wooden minesweeper with a complement of three Officers two Chiefs, three POs, twenty three ratings and no spare bunks.

She was a neatly built ship of 700 tons. Twin screws and a large generator. The sweepgear went in and out on an electric winch. Life would be very easy from that point of view. For myself, I had two seaman gunners and I could also pick a guns crew from the others. Then train them to my standards in the coming weeks.

The armament consisted of 1 x 3.50 mounted on the forecastle. 2 X 20mm AA. One either side. There were 2 x 303 light machine guns, mounted on the flag deck, 2 x Lancaster repeating rifles on the bridge, 6 X 303 Lee Enfield rifles, 3 X 45 Colts and two depth charges stored on deck. The main magazine was in the fore peak. All in all, enough work to keep me and one seaman gunner busy throughout the working day.

During the day we were busy storing ship and getting every thing shipshape and Bristol fashion, as befits a ship of the Royal Navy.

Finally we were, to all intents and purposes, ready for sea. First came the sea trials, then it was up the Hudson River to West Point. Although this is the famous Officer Training Academy for the U.S. Army, during the War years it was also a storage dump for ammunition.

After taking on our deadly cargo, we returned back down the river, passing on our way, the infamous Sing Sing Prison, and also Grant's Tomb.

We docked at Staten Island. This was to be our last stop before leaving the great American continent. A bar that we frequented here was called 'Pop's Bar'. He was a sprightly man of about seventy years of age and whenever a fracas broke, and they often did, old Pop would climb upon the bar,

A War Remembered

armed with a baseball bat and cheerfully crack anyone's head that went anywhere near him. Not that we did. He made a comical sight all the same.

It was a wet and dreary morning when we at last left our berth at Staten Island, New York. The time was 0630 hrs. As we let go our own ropes, we slipped out to sea, with a new crew member. I found a kitten sheltering under the ropes so I threw her on board. We named her Pepsi. The entire crew cared for and raised her until she grew into a fine cat, loved by all the men, including the Captain.

She became part of the ship and perhaps helped to weld together this happy band of sailors. She spread her favours evenly and would snuggle around our necks in the comfort of the Mae West lifebelts that were compulsory at sea. In rough seas, she would adjust to the roll of the ship just like the rest of us and from the start she was house trained.

When in harbour, even if we were outboard in a trot of four ships, she would go ashore and return to the 2188 after her night of courting. This wonderful animal gave birth to several litters of kittens in the mess deck and all of us acted like expectant fathers, with the fuss we made and the devotion we had for her.

On leaving Canada for home, our Pepsi didn't return to the ship. There were many lumps in many throats. Although no one would admit it, a sadness spread throughout the ship. Perhaps she thought this was her homeland, or did someone detain her

knowing that we were sailing? We all hoped and prayed that someone somewhere would look after her with the same love and attention that we had done.

The crew, by now had made their own little groups. We were all blooded in mine warfare. A good number of them had been fishermen before the start of hostilities, so seamanship was of the highest standard. We did our duty. We obeyed our Officers and senior rates, not from a strict naval point of view, but out of respect and a great feeling of loyalty.

Loyalty has to start somewhere. I think the seeds of ours started in a small bar in Boston, Mass. The Silver Dollar. On this particular night, a brawl started over nothing and a reason for not pitching in with your shipmates never existed. The U.S. Marines and Navy mixed it up with us and a real battle took place. It raged from the club, half way around the square and down a subway. A local policeman was heard to remark: "Let the silly b......s fight it out. We'll clean up afterwards."

Some time later, the Captain came to bail the battered crew out of the Boston nick. We must have looked a sorry state, lined up, heads bowed and our uniforms in various states of damage. The Police Sergeant demanded that we be punished and the skipper assured him that we would all be confined to the ship for five days. He added, with a twinkle in his eye that he would make sure that all of us complied with this punishment. He omitted to tell the Sergeant that we were sailing the following morning. We were to spend five days at sea.

The skipper never queried the fight or how and who had started it, but by his standing up for us, we knew we had a treasure in this wiry man. The sort of Captain every seaman longed to serve with. He proved his worth many times over the next few years we were together.

We sailed from Boston to Halifax, Nova Scotia, on the west coast of Canada. We were en-route for home, but the enemy laid a minefield just outside the harbour, thereby blocking the entrance to Bedford Basin. A starting point for the vital supply convoys.

The Canadians were not well up on minesweeping, so the hierarchy decided that the flotilla that was in Halifax at the time, would be seconded to the RCN to deal with this problem. The flotilla consisted of four ships. The 2188 was one of them. We made many friends in this large seaport, as we did across in Dartmouth, where we were based.

Nova Scotia at this period in time was a dry state, and although we all had the liquor controls licence to draw monthly rations, this usually went on the first day of issue. However, it wasn't long before our resourceful lads found a regular supply.....at the local bootlegger's.

The real beer was quite expensive, but the home-made hooch, lovingly distilled in a bathtub was cheap. We called it 'Kick-a-poo joy juice.' It was deadly, but our Taff Cousin said it was 'screech'. He loved it. One was enough for anyone. I reckon they could have run aircraft engines on it.

During the winter months, with the snow piled high everywhere during an illegal bootleggers party, in a three story building, some members of the crew were enjoying themselves, when there was a loud banging on the door and a voice proclaimed very loudly: "Open up. Mounted police."

You should have seen the panic, as sailors tumbled from bedroom windows and plunged head first into snow drifts. We found out later that the police weren't all that bothered at our illicit drinking but did this exercise every so often, just for laughs. They certainly had plenty to laugh at that night. What a sight it must have made.

The Halifax Minefield was cleared and before we had time to relax, the Germans had laid another one, outside St. Johns, Newfoundland. We were ordered to go there and deal with it, as this remote port was also of importance to the allied convoys.

Our first impression of Newfoundland was one of bleak desolation. The towering, brooding cliffs, enclosing a land locked harbour. After navigating the narrow channel, the town came into view. It consisted of one main street, Water Street. Along its length were some stores, cafe's, a cinema and two pubs. On one side of the harbour was a cod-liver oil factory and a fish market. This is where they chose to berth the flotilla.

Once the minefield had been cleared, we made our way back through several miles of pack ice to Canada, thus avoiding getting frozen in for the winter.

A re-fuelling stop was made at Horta Feuhel in the Portugese island of the Azores. Due to the fact that Portugal was a neutral country, we were not allowed ashore, just to avoid any trouble with the German nationals living there. A berth was provided, as were fuel and water.

From this pretty island, we progressed to Londonderry in Northern Ireland and after just a brief stop over, we sailed back home, arriving at Swansea. We had been away from home for sixteen months. Leave was the main topic on the mess deck.

When the powers that be refused us shore leave, without even giving us a reason, it caused quite a stir. After the threat of a mutiny and many heated talks between our Captain and the Base Commander, they relented and gave us six days. It should have been twenty six. However, the reason for our short spell at home, became apparent on the 6th June 1944, when the Invasion of Europe commenced.

The 2188 played her part in this epic moment of our history. We plied our skills around Omaha Beach and around the Cherbourg Peninsula. We took part in the Battle of Walcrern Island and completed the massive task of clearing the River Scheldt into Antwerp. A vital port for the Allied Armies.

The way to victory led us through the coastal ports of France, Belgium, Holland and then Germany. We celebrated V.E. Day moored in the harbour of Cuxhaven. The charts of the minefields were now in our hands and it became a straight forward task clearing them.

The final port for myself was Imjuden, Holland, and by now, most of the original crew had been replaced. In fact, I was the last of the original crew to leave. Our great skipper and the 1st Lieutenant, Lt. Mckay, were to stay on and bring the ship back to the U.K. I left in the forenoon and went to the wardroom to bid farewell to the Captain. We just looked at each other and shook hands. All he said was: "It's been a long time." The clasp of our hands said the rest. Words weren't needed.

HMBYMS 2188, was broken up at Grimsby in 1970, but the spirit of the men that made her alive will always be there. She was a stout ship. A happy and therefore, clean and efficient ship and her crew were the best mates a man could wish to have. After all, we were in a man's world and in a very close knit community, so it would only have needed one bad apple in the barrel to make life difficult. 2188 never had that problem. God bless them all."

W. J. DAVIES. NEWPORT. GWENT.

Author's Request

The author; in memory of the hardships suffered by many of the contributors to this book, in times of War, has set up an appeal fund in aid of Cancer Research at the Christie Hospital. Any readers wanting to make a donation, can do so by filling in the form below and sending their cheque/postal order payable to THE CHRISTIE HOSPITAL (WAR MEMORIES) to:-

THE CHRISTIE HOSPITAL APPEALS DEPT.
WILMSLOW ROAD
MANCHESTER
M20 4BX

WAR MEMORIES DONATIONS

NAME _____

ADDRESS _____

_____

_____ POSTCODE _____

AMOUNT DONATED _____

Thank you for your contribution towards Cancer Research at The Christie Hospital